CITYSPOTS
REIMS

Thomas Cook

D1421308

WHAT'S IN YOUR GUIDEBOOK?

Independent authors Impartial up-to-date information from our travel experts who meticulously source local knowledge.

Experience Thomas Cook's 165 years in the travel industry and guidebook publishing enriches every word with expertise you can trust.

Travel know-how Thomas Cook has thousands of staff working around the globe, all living and breathing travel.

Editors Travel-publishing professionals, pulling everything together to craft a perfect blend of words, pictures, maps and design.

You, the traveller We deliver a practical, no-nonsense approach to information, geared to how you really use it.

ABOUT THE AUTHOR

Natasha Edwards moved to Paris for all the wrong reasons in 1992 and is still there, in between seeking out obscure corners of France and art exhibitions everywhere from disused boatyards to Champagne cellars. A former editor of *Time Out Paris*, in addition to writing guidebooks, she writes regularly on art, design, food and travel for, among others, *Condé Nast Traveller*, the *Daily Telegraph*, *Design Week* and *Elle Decoration*.

CITYSPOTS
REIMS

Natasha Edwards

Written by Natasha Edwards

Published by Thomas Cook Publishing
A division of Thomas Cook Tour Operations Limited
Company registration No: 3772199 England
The Thomas Cook Business Park, 9 Coningsby Road
Peterborough PE3 8SB, United Kingdom
Email: books@thomascook.com, Tel: +44 (0)1733 416477
www.thomascookpublishing.com

Produced by The Content Works Ltd
Aston Court, Kingsmead Business Park, Frederick Place
High Wycombe, Bucks HP11 1LA
www.thecontentworks.com

Series design based on an original concept by Studio 183 Limited

ISBN: 978-1-84848-082-7

First edition © 2009 Thomas Cook Publishing
Text © Thomas Cook Publishing
Maps © Thomas Cook Publishing/PCGraphics (UK) Limited

Series Editor: Lucy Armstrong
Production/DTP: Steven Collins

Printed and bound in Spain by GraphyCems

Cover photography (Reims Cathedral) © Iconotec/Alamy

CONTENTS

SYMBOLS KEY

The following symbols are used throughout this book:

ⓐ address ☎ telephone ⓦ website address ⓛ opening times
ⓝ public transport connections ⓘ important

The following symbols are used on the maps:

ℹ️	information office	▪️	points of interest
✈️	airport	◯	city
➕	hospital	◯	large town
🛡️	police station	○	small town
🚌	bus station	=	motorway
🚉	railway station	—	main road
✝️	cathedral	—	minor road
❶	numbers denote	—	railway
	featured cafés & restaurants		

Hotels and restaurants are graded by approximate price as follows:
£ budget price **££** mid-range price **£££** expensive

Abbreviations used in addresses:

av.   avenue
blvd boulevard
pl.   place (square)

● *Aerial view of Reims from the Cathedral*

Introduction

Traditionally, two things bring visitors to Reims: Champagne and culture. The city's best-known selling points are all things bubbly on the one hand and the magnificent Gothic cathedral on the other. But there is much more to discover here. Reims' cultural spectrum ranges from Roman remains and the Romanesque Basilique Saint-Rémi to the 20th-century art deco architecture that symbolises its resurgence from near destruction in World War I. This is combined with the appeal of a lively provincial city boasting excellent restaurants and a dynamic music and performing arts scene.

With a population of 190,000, Reims is the biggest city in the Champagne-Ardennes region, though curiously not its administrative capital (which is the much smaller Châlons-en-Champagne). If it until recently had a reputation for sleepy complacency (which some might call relaxed charm), there's been a definite sense of renewal since the arrival in 2007 of the TGV high-speed train, which has brought the city to within just 45 minutes' travelling time of Paris. Not only are the Rémois now commuting regularly to the capital, but there are also a growing number of Parisians coming out to Reims. Derelict industrial premises behind the railway are due to be redeveloped and a whole new district is set to spring up around the second TGV station, Champagne-Ardenne, with offices and hotels on what is currently a greenfield site.

Like many French cities, Reims is in the process of constructing a new tramway. Due to open in 2011, it should improve connections between the outskirts and the city centre and reduce reliance on car transport, while beautifying its route with repaving and tree planting. Other ambitious projects include the Coulée Verte, which is a public footpath alongside the canal across the conurbation, and the future diversion of the A4 motorway, an eyesore that currently bisects the town. The eventual fruits of an architectural competition launched in 2008 will surely boost the considerable appeal of this renascent city.

◆ Reims with its cathedral and mixture of architectural styles

When to go

Reims is an all-year city, but it's best to visit in summer when days are longest and you can make the most of its abundant café terraces and summer festivities.

SEASONS & CLIMATE

Reims has a northern temperate climate that's also slightly continental; summers can get pretty hot (though the average temperature in July is a pleasant 18.2°C, or 65°F) and winters can be chilly. Morning fog and rain are common in autumn and winter, although the former can be a lovely time to tour the vineyards.

ANNUAL EVENTS

January

Fête de la Saint-Vincent The Sunday after 22 January brings a celebration of the patron saint of winemakers.

February

Rallye Monte-Carlo Historique Vintage cars begin the race that leads eventually to Monaco. ❶ 03 26 47 34 76

March & April

Festival Méli'môme An imaginatively programmed festival of music, contemporary dance, theatre and storytelling for children. ❶ 03 26 09 33 33 ⓦ www.meli-mome.com

April

Europuces A huge annual antiques fair and flea market at

the Parc des Expositions on the southern edge of the city.
ⓐ Rue St-Léonard ☎ 03 26 02 04 06

May
Interpol'art A week dedicated to the detective novel, with debates, book signings and short films. ⓦ www.interpolart.com
La Nuit des Musées Special night-time openings and events in museums across the city. ⓦ http://nuitdesmusees.culture.fr

June
Fête de la Musique Free open-air concerts celebrate the country's national music day, on 21 June. ⓦ www.fetedelamusique.culture.fr

June & July
Les Flâneries Musicales Classical and jazz concerts, many of them free, by first-rate performers in the cathedral (see page 58)

🔺 *A return to bygone days in the Fêtes Johanniques*

and squares of Reims, plus a giant picnic concert in Parc de Champagne (see page 86). ⓦ www.flaneriesreims.com

July
Fêtes Johanniques Reims returns to the Middle Ages in memory of Joan of Arc and Charles VII, with a costumed procession to the cathedral. ❶ 03 26 82 45 66 ⓦ www.reims-fetes.com

September
Journées du Patrimoine (third weekend) France-wide heritage days with free visits to (and special openings of) historic public buildings. ⓦ www.journeesdupatrimoine.culture.fr

October
Festival Elektricity An exciting electronic music festival with concerts, DJs, VJs, choreographic experiments and related exhibitions at La Cartonnerie (see page 100), FRAC Champagne-Ardenne (see page 88), Le Manège de Reims (see page 100) and other venues. **Fête du Massif Saint-Thierry** (odd years) Big news in these parts – the traditional wine harvest festival.

November
Les BisQueers Roses Gay, trans and lesbian film, literary and theatre festival. ❶ 03 26 88 52 56 ⓦ www.exaequoreims.com

December
Reims à Scène Ouverte Poetry and literature are the inspiration for this theatre festival at La Comédie de Reims (see page 100) and other venues.

Marché de Noël Christmas market with wooden chalets on place Drouet d'Erlon: crafts, decorations, food and drink and street entertainers create a festive atmosphere.

PUBLIC HOLIDAYS
Nouvel An (New Year's Day) 1 Jan
Lundi de Pâques (Easter Monday) 13 Apr 2009, 5 Apr 2010, 25 Apr 2011
Fête du Travail (May Day/Labour Day) 1 May
Fête de la Victoire 1945 (VE Day) 8 May
Jeudi de l'Ascension (Ascension) 21 May 2009, 13 May 2010, 2 June 2011
Lundi de Pentecôte (Whit Monday) 1 June 2009, 24 May 2010, 13 June 2011
Fête Nationale (Bastille Day) 14 July
Jour de l'Assomption (Assumption Day) 15 Aug
Toussaint (All Saint's Day) 1 Nov
Armistice 1918 (Armistice Day) 11 Nov
Noël (Christmas Day) 25 Dec

On *jours fériés* (public holidays) government departments, banks, some museums, most shops and some restaurants are closed; but some holidays are more widely observed than others, notably 1 January, 1 May, 14 July and 25 December. If a public holiday falls on a Thursday or Tuesday, many people like to *faire le pont* (bridge over) and take a four-day weekend.

Making bubbles

Grapes had been grown for centuries on the chalk slopes around Reims, but it took know-how and some astute marketing to turn the local wine into celebratory fizz. Dom Pérignon, a Dominican monk and cellar master of Hautvillers Abbey near Epernay, is credited with the idea of blending juices, introducing a second fermentation and using corks to transform what had been a rather acidic still wine with a slight sparkle into bubbly. La Veuve (widow) Cliquot added the technique of *remuage* (riddling), by which bottles are gradually rotated and tilted to remove the yeasty sediment so that the liquid becomes crystal clear. Louise Pommery, another widow, introduced guided tours around her cellars, while Eugène Mercier, a marketing genius, showed off a gigantic vat at the 1879 Great Exhibition, took clients up for tastings in hot air balloons and had the foresight to build his cellars next to the railway.

Modern Champagne production is strictly regulated: just three grape varieties are allowed – black-skinned Pinot Noir and Pinot Meunier and green-skinned Chardonnay. These are grown in some 300 communes in the Marne, Aisne and Aube *départements* (regions), and the best are classified Grand Cru. All must be harvested by hand. Most Champagne is a blend of all three grape varieties from different parcels of land and years. This maintains a consistent house style, but it can be made from just one variety (as in delicate, summery Blanc des Blancs) or just one year's harvest. The big houses who dominate production may use juice from hundreds of different patches of land, whereas some small growers may have just a tiny, precious clutch of vines that they vignify themselves, or sell to wine houses or cooperatives.

🔴 *Champagne has almost mythical status in Reims*

It's well worth touring at least one Champagne house to understand the conditions and techniques that make this wine special. If you do, note that the chalk cellars – some of them in spectacular Roman quarries – are kept at a constant and chilly 10–12°C (50–53.6°F), so wear warm clothing whatever the season.

And, just so you know what you're buying: Demi-Sec is semi-sweet; Blanc de Blancs is made only from white Chardonnay grapes; Millésimé is a vintage wine made with grapes from a single year; Rosé (pink) is Champagne made by adding some red wine.

History

Although Reims seems to have put in its first significant appearance in around 80 BC as an early Gaulish settlement of the Remses tribe, it really established itself on the map a few years later as Roman Durocortorum. At its peak in the third century AD, it was capital of the province of Belgica and one of the largest cities in the Roman Empire, with 50,000 inhabitants. Durocortorum declined somewhat with the disintegration of the Empire and subsequent barbarian activities but was still important enough to be a bishopric. Its status stood it in good stead when Frankish warrior Clovis, first Merovingian king, converted to Christianity and was baptised in the city's cathedral by Bishop Rémi (see page 85).

In 816 Louis I the Pious was crowned in Reims, beginning a tradition that continued up to Charles X in 1825 and earning the town its prestige as the Ville des Sacres, with the ceremony which conferred the divine right of kings. The most famous coronation was that of Charles VII in 1429 during the Hundred Years War, when he rode into the town – then controlled by the Burgundians, allies of Henry V of England – with Joan of Arc at his side for some muscle, in a bid to proclaim his legitimacy to the throne.

During the Middle Ages, the Champagne region was known for its important trade fairs, especially at Troyes and Provins, but in Reims itself the real power belonged to the church, as symbolised by the abbeys of Saint-Rémi and Saint-Niçaise and the start of work on a larger cathedral in 1211. The strong church presence encouraged a flourishing intellectual life: Reims founded its first university in the 16th century and its imposing Jesuit college in the 17th.

The 18th century brought the beginning of the formation of one of the modern city's key characteristics with the foundation of Champagne houses, who installed their cellars in Roman chalk quarries in the south of town; but the real bubbly boom began in the 19th century with improved production techniques and the arrival of the railway in 1849.

Reims was grievously bombarded during World War I. Miraculously, the cathedral was saved (albeit heavily damaged), but 80 per cent of the city was destroyed, leading to a colossal reconstruction programme in the 1920s. Bricks and mortar were far less troubled by World War II – Reims was occupied between 1940 and 1944; while the enemy presence can hardly have done a lot for the Rémois' general feel-good factor, it at least kept collateral damage to a minimum. After it was liberated, the city was thrust into history's limelight when it became the headquarters of Eisenhower's Allied command and was the place where General Jodl signed the Germans' unconditional surrender on 7 May 1945.

Postwar Reims has grown considerably, with the Champagne and cereals industries complemented by packaging and with the creation of a new university in the 1960s and a congress centre in the 1970s. In 1991, the city's architectural importance was underlined when several of its buildings – among them the Cathédrale Notre-Dame de Reims (see page 58), the Basilique Saint-Rémi (see page 84) and the Palais de Tau (see page 70) – were listed as UNESCO World Heritage sites. Even more significant than the election in 2008 of socialist mayor Adeline Hazan after 25 years of right-wing dominance in local politics was the advent in 2007 of the high-speed TGV rail link: thanks to that, Reims is ready to roll as a major tourist destination.

Lifestyle

An appreciation of food and wine are a central part of the *art de vivre* here – this is France, after all: café terraces are just as much vantage points for people-watching as they are places to have a coffee; going out for a meal and visiting morning food markets are social events as well as gastronomic ones, and the astonishing number of restaurants clustered around rue de Mars or on place Drouet d'Erlon demonstrates just how sociable the Rémois are. Indeed, while Reims has its share of out-of-town supermarkets, it stands out from some French provincial cities by the vitality of its town centre. Shops, restaurants, bars and cultural entertainment are all focused on or within the inner ring of boulevards, where much exploration can be done on foot, and festivals such as the traditional Fêtes Johanniques, the Fête de la Musique, Flâneries Musicales and the Marché de Noël (see pages 11–13) frequently animate the city's numerous squares.

With 22,000 students – including a large international contingent – at its university, management school and acclaimed art and design college, Reims certainly has a young, cosmopolitan aura. Champagne production is not simply a matter of prestige here but also an important source of employment. There is a vast gulf between the prosperous Champagne dynasties, who are among some of the wealthiest families in France and pursue correspondingly lavish lifestyles, and the rest of the population; indeed, this is a city where the local income is below the national average.

Although Reims is less than a hundred miles (and just 45 minutes) by train from Paris, the pace of life here is much slower than in the capital. Expect shops to close for two or three hours at midday and people to take time for lunch. For all its urban sheen, Reims remains firmly ingrained in its region, and the city's rural roots are never far away: no matter how urbanely you carry out that terrace-based people-watching, within a few minutes you can be out in the vineyards or on the agricultural plain.

⬤ *Take a breather with coffee or food on popular place Drouet d'Erlon*

Culture

For a relatively small city, Reims has a surprisingly adventurous cultural scene. Opera lovers are well catered for with the Grand Théâtre de Reims (see page 67), which programmes a variety of operas and operettas, along with occasional visiting ballet productions. The annual Flâneries Musicales festival (see page 11) enlivens the summer cultural scene and draws spectators from all over France with its first-rate array of orchestral concerts, chamber music, recitals and jazz concerts. Look out, too, for organ recitals at the Basilique Saint-Rémi (see page 84) and chamber music in the Musée des Beaux-Arts (see page 69).

If your tastes are more experimental, check out what's going on at the Conservatoire à Rayonnement Régional (see page 88), where concerts include radical sounds thanks to **Césaré, Centre National de Création Musicale** (ⓦ www.cesare-cncm.com), the organising body that supports contemporary composers and hosts an annual residence at the conservatoire (taken up by none other than Betsy Jolas in 2008). La Cartonnerie (see page 100) has quickly gained a reputation for its wide-ranging rock, pop and *chanson* (slushy French pop) offerings, which are complemented by workshops in computer-assisted music. The main concert hall is big enough to welcome major names, while a smaller space serves as a springboard for new talents.

La Comédie de Reims (see page 100) is highly reputed for contemporary drama, both in its own productions and in collaborations with other theatres, but if your French is not up to appreciating theatre texts then there's an exciting

◆ *Sculptures in the courtyard of the Musée des Beaux-Arts*

programme of circus and contemporary dance in the beautiful setting of Le Cirque and Le Manège de Reims (see page 100).

On the contemporary art front, the FRAC Champagne-Ardenne (see page 88) puts on shows at its own premises in the Ancien Collège des Jésuites and also organises exhibitions and residencies around the region. With a permanent collection encompassing works from the 1980s and rising younger names of the French scene, including Stéphane Calais and Adel Abdessemed, it also loans out works, making some interesting juxtapositions with the historic collections of the Musée des Beaux-Arts (see page 69). A more recent arrival is the Domaine Pommery (see page 85), which invites a different curator each summer to put on an art show in its cellars. Some spectacular works have been commissioned especially for the event. There's also a small gallery scene developing in the Boulingrin district with the **Galerie du Cardo** (🜂 27 rue Henri IV 🜁 03 26 87 58 62 🜃 www.galerie-du-cardo.fr) as its focal point.

It is increasingly hard to draw boundaries in Reims' energetic cultural scene, and you can always embrace the heterogeneity by catching interesting multidisciplinary projects in festivals such as Elektricity (see page 12), where computer technology meets electronic music, video and contemporary dance, or in art-music crossovers at the FRAC (see page 88).

▶ *Cathédrale Notre-Dame de Reims*

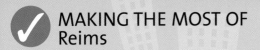

Shopping

The best shops are in the city centre. While mainstream clothing chains and shoe stores are concentrated along rue de Vesle, where there is also a branch of Parisian department store Galeries Lafayette (see page 71), the chief pleasure of shopping in Reims is its small individual boutiques, where you'll often find original, personalised choices. Try rue Thillois for cutting-edge fashion and up-and-coming labels. Other upmarket (but more staid) clothes shops can be found amid fine foodstuffs along Cours Langlet, although for the luxury designer brands, the Rémois are likely to head to Paris. Thanks to its large student population, Reims has plenty of outlets selling discount clothes and footwear, especially in the arcades off rue de Vesle. There's a more alternative ethos along rue Chanzy, where you'll find arty gallery-bookshop Rose et son roman (see page 72) and organic clothes and fairtrade gifts at Ethic et Tac (see page 71).

Interior decoration and antiques shops are concentrated on rue du Tambour and rue Colbert between place du Forum and Hôtel de Ville (see page 64). At weekends check out the antiques dealers on rue Jamin. Elsewhere, **Dapsens Auctions** (🅰 31 rue Châtivesle ☎ 03 26 47 26 37) sells an eclectic range of goods, with viewing two or three days before the sale.

Food and drink are great items to take home or for a picnic. There are several shops that sell regional products around the cathedral: as well as Champagne, other specialities include *moutarde de Reims* (Reims mustard), *vinaigre de Reims* (made from white wine matured in oak barrels), *pain d'épices* (spice cake), pink biscuits from Biscuits Fossier (see page 70) and

USEFUL SHOPPING PHRASES

What time do the shops open/close?
Á quelle heure ouvrent/ferment les magasins?
Ah kehl urr oovr/fehrm leh mahgazhang?

Can I try this on?
Puis-je essayer ceci?
Pwee zher ehssayeh cerssee?

How much is this?
Ça fait combien?
Sa fay kombyen?

My size is...
Ma taille (clothes)/ma pointure (shoes) est ...
Mah tie/mah pooahngtewr ay ...

I'll take this one, thank you
Je prends celui-ci/celle-ci, merci
Zher prohn selwee-see/sell-see, mehrsee

bouchons champenois (cork-shaped chocolates filled with
Marc de Champagne liqueur). Excellent fishmongers, butchers,
patisseries and cheese shops cluster around place du Forum
and rue de Mars. Reims' best food market is held on place
du Boulingrin on Saturday morning (🕐 06.00–13.00), but
there is also a small organic market on place Museux on
Friday (🕐 07.00–09.00), where you can often buy direct
from producers.

Eating & Drinking

Eating out is an essential part of the national way of life, and the French have different styles of restaurant to suit their mood and budget. They may go to grand gastronomic restaurants for special occasions, but it is bistros and brasseries that are the backbone of everyday convivial eating. Even bistros vary, from traditional places serving age-old recipes to new-generation venues offering market-inspired cooking and trendy presentations (think lots of frothing, layering, colourful emulsions and things presented in glasses). In Reims' art deco brasseries, the lively ambience and décor are as much a part of the experience as the cuisine, which tends towards grilled steaks and fish, and platters of shellfish. Cafés often mutate over the day, from places to pause for a coffee and croissant at breakfast, via a full-blown lunch experience and relaxed afternoon tea room to early-evening aperitif and late-night drinking haunt.

Local cuisine includes a mix of sturdy peasant recipes, like *pôtée champenoise* (a stew of ham, sausages and cabbage), and the refined Champagne sauces that accompany snails, crayfish, fish, chicken or veal. A strong *charcuterie* tradition includes *jambon*

PRICE CATEGORIES
The price ratings given in this guide indicate the approximate cost of a three-course meal for one person, not including drinks.
£ up to €25   ££ €25–40   £££ over €40

🔺 *Reims' toothsome delight:* biscuits roses

de Reims, made from pork shoulder cooked in Champagne, game pâtés and *jambon cru d'Ardennes* (cured raw ham), *boudin blanc* from Rethel and *andouillette* (chitterling sausage) from Troyes – look for those with the AAAAA quality mark, often grilled and served with a wine or mustard sauce. Another scary-sounding local speciality is *pied de porc Sainte-Ménéhoude*, a recipe for breaded pigs' trotters said to go back to medieval times – it is cooked so slowly that the bones are soft enough to eat. The region's rivers furnish freshwater fish, such as *sandre* (pike-perch) and *truite* (trout), often prepared Ardennes-style stuffed with ham, while winter game from the Ardennes forests includes *sanglier* (wild boar), *biche* (venison) and *lièvre* (hare).

USEFUL DINING PHRASES

I would like a table for ... people
Je voudrais une table pour ... personnes
Zher voodray oon tabl poor ... pehrson

Waiter/waitress
Monsieur/mademoiselle
M'syer/madmwahzel

Could I have this rare/medium/well cooked
Je le voudrais saignant/à point/bien cuit
Zher ler voodray saynyohn/ah pwan/bi-yen kwee

Does it have meat in it?
Est-ce que ce plat contient de la viande?
Essker ser plah kontyang der lah veeahngd?

I am vegetarian
Je suis végétarien/végétarienne
Zher swee vehjaytaryan/vehjaytaryanne

Where are the toilets, please?
Où sont les toilettes, s'il vous plaît?
Oo son leh twahlet, seel voo pleh?

May I have the bill, please?
L'addition, s'il vous plaît?
L'adission, seel voo pleh?

EATING & DRINKING

Cheese is traditionally served before dessert. Local varieties include creamy white Chaource, ash-covered Cendrée de Champagne and pungent Langres, with a sticky orange rind matured in Marc de Champagne liqueur. Bubbly also gets into sorbets and *sabayons* (alcoholic fruit *gratins*), while *biscuits roses*, Reims' crunchy pink boudoir biscuits, appear in many local desserts, such as creamy fruit charlottes and frozen ice cream soufflés.

The traditional French meal consists of an *entrée* (starter), *plat* (main course) and *dessert*, perhaps with a cheese course before the dessert. However, it is also perfectly acceptable, especially at lunch, to just order an *entrée* and *plat* or *plat* and *dessert*. Smarter restaurants may well also serve *amuse-gueules* (appetisers) before the starter and chocolates or *mignardises* (sweet nibbles) with the coffee; and may have *dégustation* (tasting) menus offering a larger number of smaller dishes to sample the chef's style.

Many restaurants have various *menus à prix-fixes* (set-price menus), especially at lunch, when they are often very good value. A service charge of 12 to 15 per cent is included in restaurant bills, so any extra tip is purely optional.

Restaurants typically serve from 12.00 to 14.00 or 14.30 and 19.30 or 20.00 to around 22.00; trendy bar-restaurants and brasseries frequently serve until later, especially on Friday and Saturday nights. Small chef-run restaurants often close one or two days a week and may also close in August.

Whereas in most of France Champagne is considered a drink for aperitif time or weddings, here it is perfectly acceptable to lubricate an entire meal with bubbly, though you'll find wines from all over France on wine lists as well as local still red Bouzy, rosé des Riceys and even beer from the Ardennes.

Entertainment & nightlife

Thanks to the city's big student population, nightlife in Reims tends to focus on bars and pubs. The evening often starts off in place Drouet d'Erlon, where the huge choice of bars and brasseries means there's something to suit all ages and tastes: here you'll find the latest fashionable spot packing in the students with a tempting happy hour, Latin or Caribbean joints, relaxed cocktail lounges and sophisticated seafood restaurants. Many of these places are open all day, offering inexpensive food at lunch and cocktails, tapas and sometimes DJs by night; many of them stay open until two or three in the morning, especially at weekends. The trendy spots sometimes have a short shelf life – the *rentrée* (September's back to work or place of learning) usually brings a fair share of face changes around the square, but it suffices to follow (or not) the crowds to identify the current in-vogue establishment.

Cinema remains a passion in France, and again place Drouet d'Erlon is where you'll find the city's two cinemas. The **Gaumont Reims** (❶ 08 92 69 66 96 ❻ www.cinemasgaumontpathe.com) and the Cinéma l'Opéra (see page 62) just up the street provide 13 screens between them; films at the Gaumont are generally screened in French (VF); those at the Cinéma l'Opéra are in their original language (VO), with French subtitles for foreign films; check ❻ www.allocine.fr for programmes.

When it comes to live music, you're more likely to have to head to the outskirts, with big-name rock and *chanson* acts playing La Cartonnerie (see page 100) or the Parc des Expositions, to the south of the city. Smaller outfits and local hopefuls crop up at

● *View films in their original language at Cinéma l'Opera*

⬤ Catch live bands at the Pop Art Café

WHAT'S ON?

Look for info on what's going on in the monthly freebie *Sortir à Reims* (ⓦ www.sortirareims.com), available in bars and hotels and the weekly *L'Hebdo du Vendredi*, handed out on Fridays.

more boho bar venues, such as the Pop Art Café (see page 104) and L'Appart Café (see page 104).

True clubbing generally gets going only after midnight and goes on into the early hours – but most places only open from Thursday to Saturday. Reims' trendiest clubs, such as Guest (see page 104), like to think of themselves as elitist: the current fashion for being small but exclusive is modelled on Le Baron and Paris Paris in Paris. Don't expect to get into such places if you're part of a large group of unaccompanied men; there may also be a 'no trainers' door policy.

More offbeat forms of evening entertainment exist, too. The **Hippodrome** racetrack (ⓐ 3 av. du Président Kennedy ⓣ 03 26 08 65 29 ⓦ www.hippodromedereims.com) runs night-time trotting meetings in summer. Rollerbladers can join in the Friday night roller rally on the first Friday of each month, leaving from place du Forum for a 15 km (10 mile) circuit around town (though not for beginners). There's bowling and billiards at **Le Color Bowl 51** (ⓐ ZA du Moulin de l'Ecaille, 16 rue Nicolas Appert, Tinqueux ⓣ 03 26 08 04 97 ⓦ www.colorbowl51.com), a refreshingly uncool, kitsch venue in the suburb of Tinqueux, which offers 34 lanes, karaoke and student evenings, pizzas and a bar. That's entertainment.

Sport & relaxation

SPECTATOR SPORTS

Reims' football team Stade de Reims knew its glory days between 1948 and 1962, when it won the French league four times and the French cup twice. More recently, it has been lingering in the second division but is hoping that the recent inauguration of the 22,000 capacity **Stade Delaune** (ⓐ Chaussée Bocquaine ⓦ www.stade-de-reims.com) will trigger a reversal of fortune.

PARTICIPATION SPORTS

There's a concentration of sporting facilities just across the canal from the centre, where you'll find the public swimming pools (see opposite), ice rink and the football stadium (see above). Joggers head to **Parc Léo Lagrange** (ⓐ Chaussée Bocquaine) or along the banks of the canal to keep in form, while the annual **Reims à Toutes Jambes** (ⓦ www.ratj.fr) is a popular autumnal event, combining a marathon, semi-marathon and family fun run.

Golf

Golf de Reims Eighteen-hole golf course, 15 km (10 miles) from Reims that's open to non-members. ⓐ Châteaux des Dames de France, Gueux ⓣ 03 26 05 46 10 ⓦ www.golf-de-reims.com

Swimming

Most pools are used by schools during term-time so are only open to the public early mornings, lunch times and early evenings, with longer hours during school holidays and at

weekends. Check times on the municipal sports website
Ⓦ www.rems.fr/etablissements/horaires.html. Two good pools are:
Piscine Nautilud/Patinoire Bocquaine A modern complex with
an Olympic pool, children's pool, water flume and sunbathing
terrace with paddling pool (plus an adjoining ice rink).
ⓐ 41 chaussée Bocquaine Ⓣ 03 26 82 60 00 Ⓝ Bus: G, H
Piscine Talleyrand A small art deco pool right in the town centre.
ⓐ 41 rue Talleyrand Ⓣ 03 26 47 56 18 Ⓝ Bus: A, C, D, J, T

RELAXATION

Zone Zen Spa The spa at the Grand Hôtel Europe uses high-class
Pevonia natural marine and plant-based products for massages,
facials and hydrotherapy. ⓐ 29 rue Buirette Ⓣ 03 26 47 22 33
Ⓦ www.zonezenspa.fr Ⓛ By appointment Mon–Sat

▲ *Treat yourself to a relaxing soak at the Zone Zen Spa*

Accommodation

With one or two exceptions, Reims' hotels have yet to go through the style renewal that its restaurants have experienced. There are plenty of inexpensive options, but most seem to have got stuck somewhere in the 1970s, with functional rooms and few design considerations. However, the combination of a large congress clientele and the demand generated by tourists means that even quite grotty places seem to get by very nicely, so the city can easily be fully booked. The tourist office can help if you arrive without a reservation and has an online booking service (see ⓦ www.reims-tourisme.com).

HOTELS

Grand Hôtel du Nord £ Functional yet clean with rooms that are gradually being spruced up, though beware extremely thin walls. ⓐ 75 pl. Drouet d'Erlon (The Cathedral District) ⓣ 03 26 47 39 03 ⓦ www.hotel-nord-reims.com

Hôtel Azur £ Located on a side street near the town hall, this small, family-run hotel has been tastefully redecorated with sunny colours and new bathrooms. ⓐ 9 rue des Ecrevées (The

PRICE CATEGORIES
The price ratings given in this guide are based on the average cost of a double room per night, not including breakfast.
£ up to €75   ££ €75–180   £££ over €180

Cathedral District) ☎ 03 26 47 43 39 ⓦ http://hotelazurreims.free.fr
❶ Closed Sun night

Hôtel Bristol £ The Bristol is one of the more characterful hotels on place Drouet d'Erlon, with a chandelier in the hall and good-sized rooms furnished with antiques. ⓐ 76 pl. Drouet d'Erlon (The Cathedral District) ☎ 03 26 40 52 25 ⓦ www.bristol-reims.com

Hôtel de la Cathédrale £ This attractive, small hotel down the street from the cathedral has a homely feel, pretty rooms and a faithful clientele, so reserve ahead. ⓐ 20 rue Libergier (The Cathedral District) ☎ 03 26 47 28 46 ⓦ www.hotel-cathedrale-reims.fr

Hôtel Crystal £ Reached down a curious corridor off place Drouet d'Erlon, the plus here is the flowery courtyard garden, where you can eat breakfast in summer. Inside is provincial yet comfortable. Free Wi-Fi. ⓐ 86 pl. Drouet d'Erlon (The Cathedral District) ☎ 03 26 88 44 44 ⓦ www.hotel-crystal.fr

Hôtel Latino £ Eleven festively coloured rooms above a lively bar-restaurant make this a fun option amid Reims' generally traditional hotel range. Attractions include flat-screen TV, free Wi-Fi and walk-in showers. ⓐ 33 pl. Drouet d'Erlon (The Cathedral District) ☎ 03 26 47 48 89 ⓦ www.latinocafe.fr

Best Western Hôtel de la Paix ££ The pick of the central hotels has a stunning modern design by Martine Poulet. Rich colours and Ligne Roset and Moroso furnishings feature in a design scheme that cleverly unites an art deco building and its modern extension around a surprising Renaissance chapel in the courtyard garden. Facilities include an indoor pool, gym, bar and a link to the Restaurant Café de la Paix (see page 78). ⓐ 9 rue Buirette (The Cathedral District) ⓣ 03 26 40 04 08 ⓦ www.bestwestern-lapaix-reims.com

Grand Hôtel de l'Europe ££ A comfortable, business-like hotel with a labyrinthine layout. The reception has been attractively redone, adding the town's only hotel spa on the ground floor, and rooms are reasonably sized, although upstairs corridors are looking decidedly scuffed. ⓐ 29 rue Buirette (The Cathedral District) ⓣ 03 26 47 39 39 ⓦ www.hotel-europe-reims.com

Hôtel Porte Mars ££ Overlooking the Porte de Mars, 24 bedrooms (most air-conditioned) come predominantly in pink, as does the cheerful fuschia-coloured bar with open fire in winter. ⓐ 2 pl. de la République (The Promenades & Outer Reims) ⓣ 03 26 40 28 35 ⓦ www.hotelportemars.com ⓝ Bus: A, C, F, K

● *Enjoy a comfortable stay at the Grand Hôtel de l'Europe*

Château Les Crayères £££ A mini-château that has the grounds and atmosphere of a country house hotel and is located next to the great Champagne houses. There's a galleried hallway, lavish bedrooms, a boudoir-like bar and one of the best restaurants in France (see page 93). ⓐ 64 blvd Henry Vasnier (The Saint-Rémi Quarter & the Champagne Houses) ⓣ 03 26 82 80 80 ⓦ www.lescrayeres.com

Grand Hôtel des Templiers £££ The amusing baronial hall sets the style of this 19th-century bourgeois residence, although the rooms are more traditional. A place for a quiet stay, plus an indoor pool. ⓐ 22 rue des Templiers (The Promenades & Outer Reims) ⓣ 03 26 88 55 08 ⓦ http://pagesperso-orange.fr/hotel.templiers

APARTMENTS

Séjours et Affaires Reims Clairmarais £ A modern 'apart-hotel' complex, with studios sleeping one or two and two-room flats sleeping up to four, all with kitchenette. An efficient option if you prefer to cater for yourself. There's a gym and the possibility of breakfast. ⓐ 25 rue Edouard Mignot (The Promenades & Outer Reims) ⓣ 03 26 07 74 63 ⓦ www.sejours-affaires.com

HOSTELS

Centre International de Séjour £ A big hostel where accommodation is in single and double rooms and rooms for up to five. Facilities include snooker, table tennis and bike hire. ⓐ Parc Léo Lagrange, Chaussée Bocquaine (The Promenades & Outer Reims) ⓣ 03 26 40 52 60 ⓦ www.cis-reims.com ⓝ Bus: H

THE BEST OF REIMS

Even if you're only here for a short time, Reims offers a heady blend of cultural heritage and places in which to experience and savour the French way of life.

TOP 10 ATTRACTIONS

- **Cathédrale Notre-Dame de Reims** A Gothic glory that's a not-to-be-missed feast of medieval sculpture and modern stained glass (see page 58)

- **Place Drouet d'Erlon** This lively square is an essential hub for a meal or drink and observing the world go by (see page 64)

- **Basilique Saint-Rémi** The city's second great church is a masterpiece of Romanesque volume as well as home to the magnificent tomb of Saint Rémi (see page 84)

- **Domaine Pommery** Champagne bottles encounter adventurous contemporary art in some of the most spectacular of Reims' underground cellars (see page 85)

🔻 *Reims' cathedral by night*

- **Palais de Tau** The elegant former bishop's palace recalls the city's prestigious past as the coronation town of France (see page 70)

- **Le Manège de Reims** This former equestrian riding school has become the centre of Reims' thriving cultural scene with its ambitious dance-focused programme (see page 100)

- **Musée des Beaux-Arts** The art museum contains gems by Cranach, Boucher, David, Monet and Vuillard, as well as the anonymous talents behind the strange canvases from the Hôtel Dieu (see page 69)

- **Bibliothèque Carnégie** The public library is a masterpiece of art deco craftsmanship and a symbol of the town's renewal after World War I (see page 67)

- **Musée de la Reddition 7 mai 1945** Discover the little known story of the end of World War II (see page 101)

- **Cryptoportique** A trip back in time in the mysterious underground passages in the forum of Roman Durocortorum (see page 62)

Suggested itineraries

HALF-DAY: REIMS IN A HURRY
Reims' Gothic cathedral (see page 58) is the glory of the city and
a symbol of its resilience after the destruction of World War I.
Admire the sculptures that cover the west front and go inside
to see the gorgeous stained glass windows by Chagall in the
apse. You'll still have time to buy a bottle of bubbly or liqueur-
filled chocolate Champagne corks at one of the shops on the
square outside.

1 DAY: TIME TO SEE A LITTLE MORE
Lunch in one of the up-and-coming bistros around place
Boulingrin and the rue de Mars, and then head to the southern
end of town to tour the impressive Champagne cellars at
Taittinger or Pommery (see pages 84 & 85).

2–3 DAYS: TIME TO SEE MUCH MORE
Visit the little-known Musée de la Reddition 7 mai 1945 (see
page 101), a fascinating time capsule of the end of World War II,
and the delicate frescoes of the Chapelle Foujita (see page 94).
Watch the scene at aperitif time from one of the terraces on
animated place Drouet d'Erlon, before catching a contemporary
dance show at Le Cirque (see page 100) or a concert at
La Cartonnerie (see page 100).

LONGER: ENJOYING REIMS TO THE FULL
Explore the area by meandering through the vineyards of the
Montagne de Reims to Epernay (see page 106), Reims' rival as

Champagne capital, and, for a quite different experience, head northeast to the Ardennes (see page 118).

● *Watch dance or enjoy the circus at Le Cirque*

Something for nothing

Even if you visit Reims on a small budget, there are plenty of things you can do to explore the city. The Musée Saint-Rémi (see page 89), Musée des Beaux-Arts (see page 69) and Musée de la Reddition 7 mai 1945 (see page 101) are all free on the first Sunday of the month. At other times, you might consider getting the Pass Découverte, which, for a small sum, gives one entry to each of the municipal museums and is valid for a month and can be bought at the Office de Tourisme (see page 136).

The exterior of Reims' medieval cathedral (see page 58) is itself like a free sculpture show, with its astonishing forest of carved figures and wild beasts, while the Basilique Saint-Rémi (see page 84) and the Eglise Saint-Jacques (see page 63) all continue the town's tradition of stained glass making with some striking modern windows. Then, there are varied contemporary art shows at the FRAC Champagne-Ardenne (see page 88). Otherwise, if you're interested in modern architecture, the whole centre of Reims forms a museum of the 1920s, making it a fascinating place to stroll around to observe the variety of decorative styles. A more recent modern building, the Conservatoire à Rayonnement Régional music school (see page 88), often puts on free concerts, public auditions and master classes, while once you've paid the entrance ticket, there is also occasional free chamber music in the attractive setting of the Musée des Beaux-Arts (see page 69). Reims' renowned summer music festival Les Flâneries Musicales (see page 11) has a programme that ranges from baroque and symphony concerts to jazz and world music. And after all this culture, for the price of a coffee, you can install yourself inside

⬤ Catch a quirky street performance such as this one from a Roman orchestra

a café (remember that in French cafés drinks are usually cheaper standing up at the bar than sitting down at a table) or on a pavement terrace with a book or newspaper and perfect the French art of people-watching.

When it rains

The Romans showed that they knew a thing or two about Reims' unpredictable climate when they constructed the mysterious underground Cryptoportique (see page 62) at the end of the forum so that citizens could stroll about under cover. Fortunately, the Rémois have displayed similarly acute climatic awareness since then. Whatever the weather, you can happily satisfy your shopping urges in the art deco Passage Subé (see page 72) and other glass-roofed shopping arcades that lead off place Drouet d'Erlon and rue de Vesle, with merely a quick dash between them before sidling under the arches for a drink or meal in one of the square's numerous brasseries.

Although the cathedral façade, with its wealth of sculptures and gargoyles all around, has to be truly admired from the exterior, most of the city's other principal sightseeing attractions are indoors: the grandiose Palais de Tau (see page 70), where you can see some of the cathedral sculpture and coronation regalia from close up; the Musée Saint-Rémi (see page 89), which details the city's long history; and the Musée des Beaux-Arts (see page 69), with its eclectic collection that ranges from items from the late Middle Ages to modern art.

Then, of course, there are the spectacular cellars of the Champagne houses, most of which occupy kilometres of Roman quarries and long tunnels dug into the chalk, 30 m (98 ft) underground. At the same time as learning all about bubbly, you will be protected from rain, though not from damp – humidity is 90 per cent and the temperature around 11°C (52°F) all year round (making the cellars a refreshing refuge if it's too hot in summer), so bring a jumper whatever the season.

And if you just require a little shelter for getting around in the drizzle, you could always take a tour in a **Cyclopolitain** (phone ☎ 06 27 95 54 72 or check ⓦ www.cyclopolitain.com/Reims for details), one of the city's new eco-friendly electricity-assisted tricycle taxis.

◔ *Get around in the rain in a Cyclopolitain*

On arrival

TIME DIFFERENCE

Reims is on Central European Time, one hour ahead of Greenwich Mean Time. Daylight saving applies: clocks go forward by one hour in spring and back one hour in autumn, on the same dates as in the UK.

ARRIVING

By rail

Reims is served directly by high-speed TGV in just 45 minutes from Paris and 1 hour, 25 minutes from Lille; some trains arrive at the station **Champagne-Ardenne TGV** (ⓐ Nouvelle Route de Sacy, Bezannes ① 3635 or 08 92 35 35 35) in the countryside 5 km (3 miles) outside Reims; others at the **Gare de Reims** (ⓐ Pl. de la Gare ⓦ www.gares-en-mouvement.com), right in the city centre: cross the Promenades in front of the station car park to reach place Drouet d'Erlon.

By road

Reims is 145 km (90 miles) from Paris by A4 motorway, which passes right through the eastern side of town – take exits 23 (Reims Centre), 24 (Cathédrale) or 25 (Saint-Rémi) for the town centre – and is 270 km (170 miles) from Calais on the A26, which connects with the A4 west of the city.

FINDING YOUR FEET

Reims is a relatively compact place: most of the main sights, places to eat and shops are in the centre. For an insight into how the city works, head straight for place Drouet d'Erlon, its busiest square. The locals are used to visitors, and many people speak at least some English; but it's always polite to at least try out a few basic French words. Sallying forth with a cheery *bonjour* or unveiling a coy *merci* will generate goodwill.

ORIENTATION

The city centre is ringed by a series of busy boulevards, bordered to the north by the grassy Promenades which divide the historic centre from the train station, and bordered on the west by the triple band of the Canal de l'Aisne, River Vesle and A4 autoroute. Pedestrianised place Drouet d'Erlon, which is packed with hotels, cafés, brasseries, shops and cinemas is a first port of call

● *One of Reims' two train stations – Champagne-Ardenne TGV*

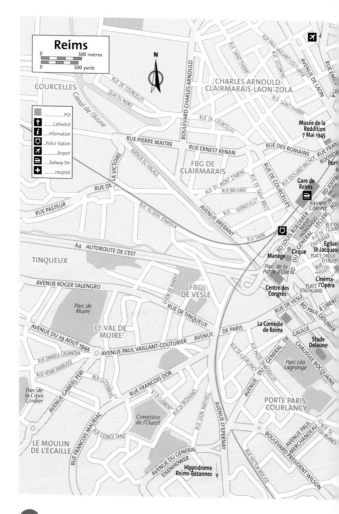

for many visitors; running east-west south of here along rue de Vesle and its continuation from rue Carnot is Reims' main shopping thoroughfare; the cathedral (see page 58) is located on a paved parvis just south of here – its twin towers can be spotted from many parts of town. South of the cathedral district, the rue Gambetta leads towards Basilique Saint-Rémi (see page 84) and the district around the southern boulevards where many of the Champagne houses are located. If you're visiting on business, **Reims Congress Centre** (ⓐ 12 blvd Général Leclerc ⓣ 03 26 77 44 44 ⓦ www.reims-evenements.fr) is located in the Parc de la Patte d'Oie at the western end of the Promenades, an easy walk from the station; the Parc des Expositions is on the southern edge of town.

If you're just here for a short time, you may want to take an open-topped bus tour organised by the tourist office (see page 136), which is located beside the cathedral. The tourist office also rents out six different audio guides in several languages for visiting the city centre architecture and the town's UNESCO World Heritage listed sights.

GETTING AROUND

The city centre between the Promenades and the cathedral (see page 58) is partly pedestrianised and most easily tackled on foot, but you may want to use public transport to get to the Basilique Saint-Rémi (see page 84) and the Champagne houses in the southern half of town, as well as to some of the cultural venues located outside the central zone. The city has an efficient network of local buses run by TUR (Transport Urbains de Reims), labelled A-Z, and two Citadine buses running Monday to Saturday only

IF YOU GET LOST, TRY...

Do you speak English?
Parlez-vous anglais?
Pahrlay-voo ahnglay?

Could you tell me the way to...
Comment fait-on pour aller à ...
Kohmohn feyt-ohn poor al-lay ah ...

Could you point to it on my map?
Pouvez-vous me le montrer sur la carte?
Poo vay voo muh ler montray soor lah kart?

in opposite directions from the train station. These do a circuit of the town centre, taking in many of the tourist sights. Most bus lines run from around 06.00 to around 20.30; there are also five night lines that run until midnight. Single bus trips cost €1, allow one change of bus within 60 minutes and can be bought from the driver, as can a one-day bus pass for €3, covering all local routes and the Citadines; other travel passes can be bought from the **TUR office** (❷ 6 rue de Chanzy ❶ 03 26 88 25 38 ⓦ www.tur.fr).

Reims is currently in the process of constructing a new tramway (see ⓦ www.tramwaydereims.fr), which is due to come into service in April 2011, running through the town centre along Cours Langlet and rue de Vesle and making some of the outer reaches of the city more accessible. In the meantime, however, be prepared for

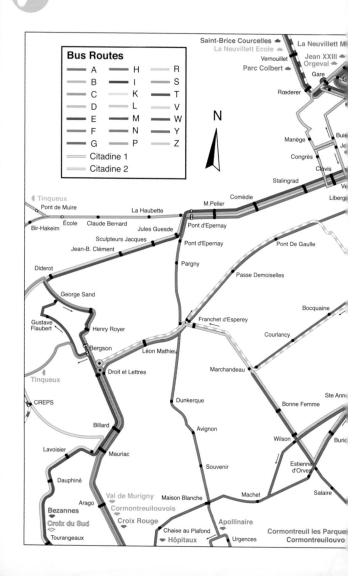

a certain amount of disruption and traffic diversions caused by road works and archaeological digs during its construction.

With virtually no hills, Reims is also an ideal city for cycling around. Bikes can be hired from **Holiday Bikes** (ⓐ Cour de la Gare ⓣ 03 26 82 57 81 ⓦ www.holiday-bikes.com) located inside the Ada car hire offices by the train station. Taxis can be hailed in the street or found at the station. To reserve a taxi call **Les Taxis de Reims** (ⓣ 03 26 47 05 05).

In this guide, for listings where no public transport connections are given, you can assume that they are most easily reached on foot.

CAR HIRE

Most main car rental firms have outlets in the forecourt of Reims station or on the nearby boulevards. If you're travelling by train or plane, there are often good rates if you rent a car at the same time as booking your ticket. To rent a car, drivers should have had a licence for at least two years and generally be over 23; be sure to bring your driving licence, passport, credit card and proof of your address with you.

Ada ⓐ Cour de la Gare ⓣ 03 26 50 08 40 ⓦ www.ada.fr

Avis ⓐ Cour de la Gare ⓣ 03 26 47 10 08 or 08 20 61 17 05 ⓦ www.avis.com

Europcar ⓐ 76 blvd Lundy ⓣ 08 25 04 52 82 ⓦ www.europcar.com

Hertz ⓐ 26 blvd Joffre ⓣ 03 26 47 98 78 ⓦ www.hertz.fr

Rent-a-Car ⓐ Cour de la Gare ⓣ 03 26 77 87 77 ⓦ www.rentacar.fr

❍ *Grand Théâtre de Reims*

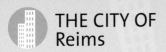

THE CITY OF
Reims

The Cathedral District

The town centre clusters around the magnificent cathedral, symbol of its survival after the trauma of World War I. But if the cathedral is Reims' emotional heart, then busy place Drouet d'Erlon is its pulse. Behind here, many of the streets follow the old Roman grid, with broad rue de Vesle running east-west and a north-south axis falling through Boulingrin market square and place du Forum.

SIGHTS & ATTRACTIONS

Cathédrale Notre-Dame de Reims

The cathedral was begun in 1211, adopting the new Gothic style, and was largely complete by the end of the century. This has given it a rare unity of style, with its twin towers, great rose windows and extraordinary wealth of decoration. Thousands of sculptures cover the west front with its three doorways and the row of giant Kings of Judah high above the rose window. The cathedral was badly shelled in World War I and has equally suffered from erosion, necessitating a near continuous process of restoration. Even the inside of the portals are sculpted, with rows of niches containing statues of saints; but the interior strikes one above all with the impression of height, accentuated by the relative sobriety and narrowness of the nave. At the east end, beautiful stained glass designed by Marc Chagall in 1974 provides a blaze of colour in a flowing composition depicting Abraham, the Crucifixion and the story of the cathedral. In the transept, the 'vigneron's window' shows the different stages of

🔺 *Ornate detail on the Gothic façade of Cathédrale Notre-Dame de Reims*

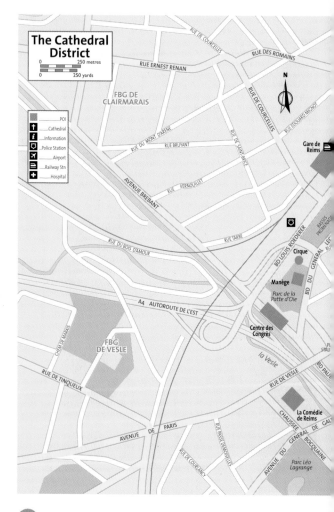

The Cathedral District

0 — 250 metres
0 — 250 yards

POI
Cathedral
Information
Police Station
Airport
Railway Stn
Hospital

RUE DE COURCELLES
RUE DES ROMAINS
RUE ERNEST RENAN
FBG DE CLAIRMARAIS
RUE DE COURCELLES
RUE EDOUARD MIGNOT
N
RUE DU MONT D'ARÈNE
RUE BRUYANT
RUE DE SAINT-BRICE
Gare de Reims
AVENUE BRÉBANT
RUE VERNOUILLET
RUE TARBE
BD LOUIS ROEDERER
BASSES PROMENADES
BD DU GÉNÉRAL LECLERC
RUE DU BOIS D'AMOUR
Cirque
Manège
Parc de la Patte d'Oie
A4 AUTOROUTE DE L'EST
Centre des Congrès
PL. STALI
FBG DE VESLE
la Vesle
BD PAUL
RUE DE TINQUEUX
CHAUX & MILLUS
RUE DE VESLE
La Comédie de Reims
CHAUSSÉE BOCQUAINE
AVENUE DE PARIS
RUE PASSE DEMOISELLES
AVENUE DU GÉNÉRAL DE GAU
RUE DE COURLANCY
Parc Léo Lagrange

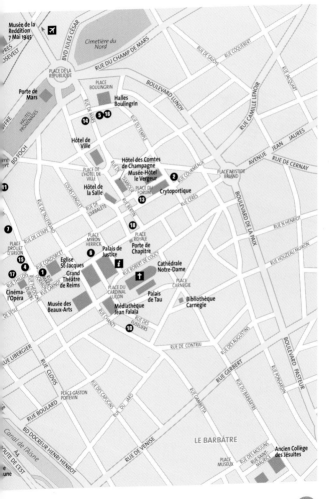

Champagne making. Be sure to walk around the outside to the east end, with its massive flying buttresses and giant lions and other beasts looming off the parapets. Pl. du Cardinal Luçon Cathedral: 07.30–19.30 except during services; tower visits: 10.00, 11.00, 14.00, 15.00, 16.00 Tues–Sat, mid-Mar–Oct. Bus: Citadine 1 & 2. Admission charge for towers

Cinéma l'Opéra

Although it's sadly in need of restoration, be sure to admire the extraordinary rue Thillois façade of this cinema, which opened in 1923. It has a style all of its own, somewhere between art nouveau and art deco, with wavy porch, floral stained glass, golden mosaics and terracotta sculptures. The modern six-screen cinema entrance is round the corner on rue Théodore Dubois. 11 rue Thillois 03 26 47 13 54

Cours Langlet

Home to some great specialist food shops, this broad street was created as part of the reconstruction of Reims with domed apartment buildings, neo-vernacular houses and the striking Maison de la Mutualité at no. 12 with floral frieze and reliefs representing different trades and crafts.

Cryptoportique

These mysterious second-century U-shaped semi-underground chambers at one end of the Roman forum probably served as some sort of meeting place and a grain store. The exterior section is now used for concerts in summer. Pl. du Forum 03 26 50 13 74 14.00–17.00 mid-June–mid-Sept Bus: Citadine 1 & 2

Eglise Saint-Jacques

A simple ancient façade conceals the oldest parish church in Reims, built in 1190. The windows were destroyed during World War I, and have been replaced by striking geometrical modern stained glass in the apse and transept. On rue Condorcet, you can see the slate-covered belfry. ⓐ Rue Marx Dormoy ⓣ 03 26 47 55 34 ⓛ 14.00–18.00 Mon, 09.00–12.00, 14.00–18.00 Tues–Sat, 17.30–19.00 Sun

Halles Boulingrin

The former market hall is a whale of a structure and a feat of reinforced concrete, with a massive parabolic vault. Empty since 1989, it is due to reopen in 2012 after restoration for use both as a food market and for cultural events. ⓐ Pl. Boulingrin Ⓝ Bus: A, C, F, K

Hôtel des Comtes de Champagne

The rare remains of a 13th-century Gothic hall stand on what was once an important medieval merchant street. The ground floor, now used for private functions by the Maison Taittinger and not open to the public, originally contained shops.
ⓐ 22 rue de Tambour Ⓝ Bus: Citadine 1 & 2

Hôtel de la Salle

Adorned with arabesque friezes and figures of Adam and Eve over the door, this restored Renaissance townhouse was built in the 16th century for a wealthy cloth merchant, and was the birthplace of Jean-Baptiste de la Salle, founder of Christian charity schools, in 1651. ⓐ 4 bis rue de l'Arbalète ⓣ 03 26 47 73 21 ⓛ Open to groups by advance reservation Ⓝ Bus: Citadine 1 & 2

Hôtel de Ville

The grandiose town hall resembles a mini château with its pitched roof, central turret, ornate façade and an equestrian sculpture of Louis XIII over the entrance. It was begun in 1627, although a shortage of funds meant it was completed only in the 19th century. The interiors were reconstructed after World War I in a blend of historic and art deco styles. Around the corner on rue de Mars, take a look at the winemaking mosaics on the former Caves Mumm. 🄰 Pl. de l'Hôtel de Ville ☏ 03 26 77 78 79 🕐 08.30–12.00, 13.00–17.00 Mon–Fri 🆆 www.ville-reims.fr 🄽 Bus: Citadine 1 & 2

Place Drouet d'Erlon

This animated pedestrianised square lined with hotels, brasseries, shops and cinemas is busy night and day. Halfway down, the Fontaine Subé is topped by a gilded winged figure of Victory, who soars into the air above allegorical statues of the Rivers Marne, Vesle, Suippe and Aisne.

Place Royale

Reims' most elegant square was laid out in 1760 with balustraded neoclassical façades around a bronze statue of Louis XV as Roman emperor. 🄽 Bus: B, C, D, E, N

Porte du Chapître

A turreted 16th-century gateway that orginally led to the canon's quarter. 🄰 Rue de Vesle 🄽 Bus: Citadine 1 & 2

◢ *The château-like Hôtel de Ville*

⬥ *Art deco galore at the Bibliothèque Carnegie*

CULTURE

Bibliothèque Carnegie

This stunning art deco library is a symbol of the city's reconstruction, financed through a $200,000 gift by American millionaire Andrew Carnegie as a gesture against the barbarity of war and inaugurated in 1928. It is beautifully restored so you can appreciate its pared-back façade, unusual drum-shaped book reserve and lavishly decorated interior. The domed entrance hall has a geometric chandelier, onyx panelling, marble mosaic scenes and a fountain symbolising 'the fountain of life, source of all science and wisdom', while pearly stained glass filters the light in the mahogany reading room. ⓐ 2 pl. Carnegie ⓣ 03 26 77 81 41 ⓛ 10.00–13.00, 14.00–19.00 Tues, Wed & Fri, 14.00–19.00 Thur, 10.00–13.00, 14.00–18.00 Sat ⓝ Bus: Citadine 1 & 2

Grand Théâtre de Reims

Only the grand neo-Renaissance stone façade with its busts of Tragedy and Comedy on either side remains of the theatre built in the 1870s; the rest was reconstructed in the 1920s in reinforced concrete, creating a splendid art deco foyer and auditorium, now used for opera, ballet, operettas and musicals. ⓐ 1 rue de Vesle ⓣ 03 26 50 03 92 ⓦ www.grandtheatredereims.com ⓛ Opening hours vary according to performances ⓝ Bus: A, B, C, D, N, K

Médiathèque Jean Falala

This striking glass and steel library on the corner of the cathedral square is the modern counterpart to the Bibliothèque Carnegie (see above) offering audio and video resources alongside books, a gallery and short films and documentary screenings in the auditorium. ❸ 2 rue des Fuseliers ☎ 03 26 35 68 00 🌐 www.bm-reims.fr ⏰ 13.00–19.00 Tues, Thur & Fri, 10.00–19.00 Wed, 10.00–18.00 Sat 🚌 Bus: A, F, G, H, T

ART DECO RECONSTRUCTION

World War I wrought terrible destruction on Reims, but it was also a spur for modernisation. At the end of the war, just 67 buildings were fit for habitation. Some were restored in such a way that their façades were preserved, but others were begun from scratch, meaning that aside from the cathedral and a handful of historic buildings, the centre of Reims is essentially a modern city. The 300 architects from all over France who were involved in the reconstruction worked in a multiplicity of styles: neo-Renaissance, classical, vernacular, late art nouveau – but art deco dominated. This was epitomised by the Bibliothèque Carnegie (see page 67), but it also marked the city's banks, shops, apartment blocks, everyday housing and streets. Rue de Talleyrand, place Drouet d'Erlon with its cinema, arcaded Passage Subé and tea room Waida (see page 74), the turreted Kodak building at 65 rue de Vesle and broad Cours Langlet, rue de Mars and rue du Temple abound in floral friezes, vertical fluting, geometrical wrought-iron balconies and banisters, mosaics and stained glass *verrières* and streamlined forms that evoked modernity.

Musée des Beaux-Arts

Occupying an 18th-century monastery, the fine art collection
is presented alongside decorative arts, occasionally juxtaposed
with contemporary art. Upstairs, along with a large collection
of 17th-century French, Dutch and Flemish paintings, highlights
include a rare set of portraits by Cranach, a lewd painting by
Boucher, David's *Death of Marat*, a whole room of paintings by
Corot and two fine landscapes by Monet. However the biggest
curiosities are the 26 late 16th-century painted canvases from
the Hôtel Dieu (old hospital); painted by anonymous artists, the
lively Biblical scenes were perhaps an inexpensive alternative to
tapestries, while providing educational and moral enlightenment.
On the ground floor, the modern collection includes Gauguins,
a gorgeous small Vuillard and paintings by Joseph Sima. ⓐ 8 rue
Chanzy ⓣ 03 26 47 28 44 ⓛ 10.00–12.00, 14.00–18.00 Wed–Mon
ⓝ Bus: A, F, G, H, T. Admission charge

Musée-Hôtel le Vergeur

With a half-timbered street façade and Renaissance courtyard,
this mansion was home for a while to the Veuve Cliquot and later
to wine merchant Hugues Krafft, who incorporated Renaissance
fireplaces and Gothic lintels from some of Reims' destroyed
buildings alongside his collection of furniture. Still arranged
like a private house, rooms capture the 19th-century bourgeois
lifestyle, while treasures include a complete set of Durer's
engravings and woodcuts. ⓐ 30 pl. du Forum ⓣ 03 26 47 20 75
ⓦ www.museelevergeur.com ⓛ Guided visits: 14.00, 15.00, 17.00
Tues–Sun; temporary exhibitions: 14.00–18.00 ⓝ Bus: Citadine 1
& 2. Admission charge

Palais de Tau

The 17th-century former bishop's palace incorporates the earlier Gothic chapel and Great Hall used for coronation banquets. Now the cathedral museum, it contains many of its original sculptures, providing a wonderful opportunity to see them closer up than you ever could *in situ*. Other exhibits include tapestries of the Life of the Virgin, the ship-shaped medieval reliquary of Saint Ursula and the coronation robes of Charles X, the last monarch to be crowned in Reims in 1825. Pl. du Cardinal Luçon 03 26 47 81 79 www.monum.fr 09.30–18.30 Tues–Sat, Apr–Sept; 09.30–12.30, 14.00–17.30 Tues–Sat, Oct–Mar Bus: Citadine 1 & 2. Admission charge

RETAIL THERAPY

Biscuits Fossier Reims' famous crunchy pink boudoir biscuits, which the Maison Fossier has been making since 1756, are sold in a suitably coloured boutique. 25 cours Langlet 03 26 47 59 84 www.biscuits-fossier.com 14.00–19.00 Mon, 09.00–19.00 Tues–Sat Bus: A, C, D, F, K, T

Cave aux Fromages Tempting cheese shop that's a source of wonderful, well-ripened farmhouse cheeses from all over France. 12 pl. du Forum 03 26 47 83 05 08.30–13.00, 15.30–20.00 Tues–Sat Bus: B, C, D, E, N, Citadine 1 & 2

Les Caves du Forum Shop specialising in wines from all over France bought direct from producers, with 900 Champagne and wine references displayed in gorgeous barrel-vaulted cellars (and

frequent tasting days). ⓐ 10 rue Courmeaux ⓣ 03 26 79 15 15
ⓦ www.lescavesduforum.com ⓛ 14.00–19.30 Mon, 09.00–12.30,
14.00–19.30 Tues–Sat ⓝ Bus: B, C, D, E, N, Citadine 1 & 2

Deleans *Ganaches*, marzipan fruit and slabs of chocolate
are displayed in a pretty panelled period shop. ⓐ 20 rue Cérès
ⓣ 03 26 47 56 35 ⓛ 14.00–19.00 Mon, 09.00–12.30 (12.00 Wed),
14.00–19.00 Tues–Sat ⓝ Bus: B, C, D, E, N

Espace d'Erlon This modern shopping arcade contains a branch
of useful book, music, photography and computer store Fnac,
its children's toy and book offshoot Fnac Eveil et Jeux, practical
supermarket Monoprix and Alice Délice, a great kitchen shop.
ⓐ 53 pl. Drouet d'Erlon ⓛ 10.00–19.30 Mon–Sat, Monoprix:
09.00–20.00 Mon–Sat ⓝ Bus: A, C, D, F, K, T, Citadine 1 & 2

Ethic et Tac Organic and fairtrade clothes and accessories prove
that ecological can be cool. ⓐ 67 rue Chanzy ⓣ 03 26 97 81 44
ⓛ 10.00–12.00, 14.00–19.00 Mon–Sat ⓝ Bus: A, F, G, H, T

Galeries Lafayette Although now a branch of the
Parisian department store, these four floors of galleries are
clustered around a vast central space. ⓐ 33–45 rue de Vesle
ⓣ 03 26 40 35 12 ⓦ www.galerieslafayette.com ⓛ 09.30–19.30
Mon–Sat, food store: 08.30–20.00 Mon–Sat ⓝ Bus: B, K, M, N,
Citadine 1 & 2

Kidnapull A tiny boutique with groovy women's labels including
ethno-chic Isabel Marant and American Vintage. ⓐ 7 rue Thillois

03 26 47 49 14 14.00–19.00 Mon, 10.00–19.00 Tues–Sat
Bus: A, C, D, F, K, T, Citadine 1 & 2

Le Parvis A wide choice of Champagne and other Reims specialities, and the possibility of a snifter on the terrace in front of the cathedral. Pl. du Cardinal Luçon 03 26 47 44 44 09.00–19.00 Bus: Citadine 1 & 2

Passage Subé This glass-roofed art deco passageway forms a crossroads between place Drouet d'Erlon and rues de l'Etape and Condorcet. Among the shops, check out the funky costume jewellery, gifts by Guess, Scooter, Lollipops and others at Diapason, well-priced clothes and accessories at G4, and childrenswear at Enfance and IKKS. Shops open 14.00–19.00 Mon, 10.00–19.00 Tues–Sat Bus: A, C, D, F, K, T, Citadine 1 & 2

Rose et son roman An arty bookshop, gallery and tea room. 78 rue Chanzy 03 26 47 30 60 10.00–12.00, 14.00–19.00 Tues–Sat Bus: A, F, G, H, T

Tandem The most cutting-edge selection of clothes and bags in Reims includes designs by Paul & Joe Sister, Vanessa Bruno, Thomas Burberry, See by Chloé and Repetto shoes. 22 rue de Thillois 03 26 05 84 32 14.00–19.00 Mon, 10.00–19.00 Tues–Sat Bus: A, C, D, F, K, T, Citadine 1 & 2

Terroir des Rois Just by the north door of the cathedral. Pick up regional specialities to take home. 8 rue Robert de Coucy 03 26 88 34 95 09.00–19.00 Bus: Citadine 1 & 2

Rue de Vesle, one of Reims' main shopping streets

TAKING A BREAK

Crêperie Louise £ ❶ A pretty crêperie and tea room that's ideal for a light lunch or an afternoon pause over salads, sweet and savoury crêpes, or waffles with caramel sauce and whipped cream. ⓐ 15 rue Marx Dormoy ❶ 03 26 78 00 61 ❶ 12.00–14.00 Mon, 12.00–22.00 Tues–Sat ⓝ Bus: A, B, C, D, F, K, M, N

Epicerie au Bon Marché £ ❷ Gourmet deli with rustic wooden shelving laden with jars of goodies and a few cheerful formica tables where you can snack on plates of cheeses and *charcuterie* or smoked salmon and wines from the Caves du Forum across the street. ⓐ 7 rue Courmeaux ❶ 03 26 03 45 29 ❶ 10.00–20.00 Mon–Sat ⓝ Bus: B, C, D, E, N, Citadine 1 & 2

Les Trois Brasseurs £ ❸ This casual micro-brasserie brews its own beers in large metal vats by the entrance. Generous salads, steaks, *choucroute* and *flammekuches* and long hours make it a useful option for a late lunch or Sunday nibbling. ⓐ 73 pl. Drouet d'Erlon ❶ 03 26 47 86 28 ❶ 12.00–23.00 Mon–Sat, 12.00–00.00 Sun ⓝ Bus: A, C, D, F, K, T, Citadine 1 & 2

Waida £ ❹ Baker and patisserie at the front and tea room behind, Waida is a local landmark where colourful macaroons and delicious fruit tarts vie for attention with the art deco glass and marquetry panelling. ⓐ 5 pl. Drouet d'Erlon ❶ 03 26 47 44 49 ❶ 07.30–19.30 Tues–Fri & Sun, 07.30–20.00 Sat ⓝ Bus: A, C, D, F, K, T, Citadine 1 & 2

Brasserie du Boulingrin ££ ❺ Lively art deco brasserie that's an institution with its banquettes and brass, where sturdy burghers enjoy classics like shellfish, offal, steaks and *gratin dauphinois*. 📍 48 rue de Mars 📞 03 26 40 96 22 🌐 www.boulingrin.fr 🕐 12.00–14.30, 19.00–23.00 Mon–Thur, 12.00–14.30, 19.00–23.30 Fri & Sat 🚍 Bus: A, C, F, K

Café du Palais ££ 6 This classic café opposite the Palais de Justice has been run by the same family since it opened in 1930, drawing local bigwigs and tourists with its banquettes, flouncy lights and art deco stained glass *verrière* for lunch on gourmet salad platters, hot *plats du jour* and homemade desserts. 📍 14 pl. Myron Herrick 📞 03 26 47 52 54 🌐 www.cafedupalais.fr 🍴 Meals: 12.00–15.00 Mon, 12.00–14.30, 19.00-21.30 Tues–Sat 🚍 Bus: A, B, C, D, N, K

AFTER DARK

RESTAURANTS
L'Apostrophe £ 7 A cavernous red-walled space, where books round the columns and old newspapers pasted over the bar recall its past as a printworks. There's a good wine list and the menu plays a world card from *salade niçoise* to *salade balinaise*, Thai kebabs to a *speculoos* apple crumble. 📍 59 pl. Drouet d'Erlon 📞 03 26 79 19 89 🌐 www.restaurant-lapostrophe.com 🕐 12.00–14.30, 19.00–23.30 (bar 10.00–03.00) 🚍 Bus: A, C, D, F, K, T, Citadine 1 & 2

Matsuri Sushi £ 8 Sit at a table or along the conveyer-belt bar and help yourself to *sushi* and *maki*. 📍 9 rue de Châtivesle 📞 03 26 86 10 10 🌐 www.matsuri.fr 🕐 12.00–14.30, 19.00–23.00 🚍 Bus: A, C, D, F, K, T, Citadine 1 & 2

⬥ *Detail of the art deco stained glass ceiling at the Café du Palais*

La Médina £ ⑨ A friendly Moroccan restaurant that serves up traditional fare in an atmospheric tented Berber interior. ⓐ 13 rue de Châtivesle ⓣ 03 26 88 43 34 ⓛ 12.00–14.00, 19.00–22.00 Tues–Thur, 12.00–14.00, 19.00–23.00 Fri & Sat ⓝ Bus: A, C, D, F, K, T, Citadine 1 & 2

La Trattoria £ ⑩ An attractive Italian restaurant not far from the cathedral serving up bruschetta, fresh pasta, *osso bucco* and veal escalopes. ⓐ 45 rue de Chanzy ⓣ 03 26 61 87 37 ⓛ 12.00–14.30, 19.00–22.00 Tues–Sat ⓝ Bus: A, F, G, H, T

Brasserie Flo ££ ⑪ With its grand staircase and wooden panelling, this superb *hôtel particulier* is great for dining in style on shellfish and updated brasserie fare. ⓐ 96 pl. Drouet d'Erlon ⓣ 03 26 91 40 50 ⓦ www.floreims.com ⓛ 12.00–15.00, 19.00–23.30 Mon–Sat, 12.00–15.00, 19.00–23.30 Sun ⓝ Bus: A, C, D, F, K, T, Citadine 1 & 2

Le Continental ££ ⑫ A classic brasserie with a big tank of lobsters and a golden tree sculpture in the middle of the dining room. Come here for seafood and regional cooking with plenty of Champagne sauces. ⓐ 95 pl. Drouet d'Erlon ⓣ 03 26 47 01 47 ⓛ 12.00–15.00, 19.00–23.00 ⓝ Bus: A, C, D, F, K, T, Citadine 1 & 2

Edgar Bistrot ££ ⑬ This stylish, modern two-storey bistro all in black and white is a hit for its relaxed, friendly staff and light, inventive take on French cuisine: perhaps trendy savoury tiramisus, sea bass on a bed of onions and carrots, scallops with chicory or *boudin blanc* from Rethel. ⓐ 2 pl. du Forum ⓣ 03 26 09 70 70 ⓛ 12.00–14.30, 19.30–22.30 Mon–Thur, 12.00–14.30, 19.30–23.30 Fri & Sat, 12.00–14.30 Sun ⓝ Bus: B, C, D, E, N, Citadine 1 & 2

Le Petit Comptoir ££ ⓮ Champagne buckets in the window set the tone at this stylish bistro, which is very popular for updated versions of bistro classics with cosmopolitan touches and rediscovered grandmotherly favourites. ⓐ 17 rue de Mars ⓣ 03 26 40 58 58 ⓛ 12.00–14.30, 19.15–22.30 Tues–Sat ⓝ Bus: A, C, F, K

Restaurant Café de la Paix ££ ⓯ Suave designer brasserie done up in slinky neo-70s Pop colours, with areas where you can sit at stools along a bar or settle back in discrete booths. Oysters, steak tartare and *choucroute garnie* are specialities ⓐ 25 pl. Drouet d'Erlon ⓣ 03 26 47 00 45 ⓦ www.restaurant-cafe-de-la-paix.fr ⓛ 12.00–23.00 ⓝ Bus: A, C, D, F, K, T, Citadine 1 & 2

Version Originale ££ ⓰ The globe-trotting menu changes daily but might go from Chinese *nems* and North African-inspired tagines to ever-so-French foie gras. Romantic candlelit setting. ⓐ 25 bis rue du Temple ⓣ 03 26 02 69 32 ⓦ www.vo-reims.fr ⓛ 12.00–14.00, 19.00–22.00 Tues–Thur, 12.00–14.00, 19.30–22.30 Fri & Sat ⓝ Bus: A, C, F, K

La Vigneraie ££ ⓱ This elegant dining room is one of Reims' most reliable addresses for the refined modern regional cooking of chef Hervé Baudier, who injects imagination and spices into dishes like duckling with blackcurrants or a fricassée of asparagus and morels. ⓐ 12–14 rue de Thillois ⓣ 03 26 88 67 27 ⓦ www.vigneraie.com ⓛ 12.00–13.30, 19.30–21.30 Tues & Thur–Sat, 19.30–21.30 Wed, 12.00–13.30 Sun ⓝ Bus: A, C, F, K

Le Millénaire £££ ⓮ Located on a pedestrian street off place du Forum, a dressy dining room and modern paintings set the scene for accomplished cooking that uses lobster, sea bass and wild mushrooms in a roll call of fine ingredients. ⓐ 4–6 rue Bertin ⓣ 03 26 08 26 62 ⓦ www.lemillenaire.com ⓛ 12.00–14.00, 19.15–21.15 Mon–Fri, 19.15–21.15 Sat ⓝ Bus: B, C, D, E, N, Citadine 1 & 2

BARS & CLUBS

Gin Pamp Definitely the place to come at happy hour, if you can make it anywhere near the bar through the student throng; or simply for a beer on one of the two pavement terraces during the day. DJs Thursday to Saturday. ⓐ 14 rue Théodore Dubois ⓣ 03 26 47 19 48 ⓛ 10.00–00.00 Mon–Thur, 10.00–02.30 Fri & Sat ⓝ Bus: A, B, C, D, F, K, M, N

Latino Café A pulsating, colourful Latin-themed bar drawing lots of giggly girls for cocktails and tapas. Live music on Thursday nights. ⓐ 33 pl. Drouet d'Erlon ⓣ 03 26 47 48 89 ⓦ www.latinocafe.fr ⓛ 08.00–03.00 ⓝ Bus: A, C, D, F, K, T, Citadine 1 & 2

Le Royalty A classic cocktail bar with a long moody interior and big squashy orange and white sofas for chilling out on the square. ⓐ 67 pl. Drouet d'Erlon ⓣ 03 26 88 52 88 ⓛ 10.00–03.00 ⓝ Bus: A, C, D, F, K, T, Citadine 1 & 2

The Saint-Rémi Quarter & the Champagne Houses

South of the Cathedral district, rue Gambetta leads down from rue Chanzy, continuing the Voie des Sacrés, the royal route taken at coronation time between the cathedral and Reims' second great UNESCO-listed church, the Basilique Saint-Rémi, once a powerful abbey. The junction of the two streets is marked by a striking modern rusty steel sundial sculpture. Today the Bourg Saint-Rémi is mainly taken up by modern housing, but the area is also home to many of Reims' Champagne houses. Clubbers and bar-crawlers will be frustrated in this area – if you don't fancy a sit-down meal, the nightlife thrills consist of little more than the conviviality of the kebab stand.

SIGHTS & ATTRACTIONS

Ancien Collège des Jésuites

At the moment you can only visit the courtyards of this beautiful 17th-century ensemble that was built as a Jesuit school. A fine example of classical baroque architecture, its chief treasures, the grand staircase and the library, will reopen only in 2012 when the whole building has been restored. The courtyard to the left of the chapel was for the Jesuit fathers. A sign indicates the entrance of the Magnanerie, a sort of charity school to educate poor girls for work as housemaids. The second courtyard for the pupils now contains the Planétarium and the FRAC Champagne-Ardenne (see pages 90 & 88). ⓐ 1 pl. Museux ⓣ 03 26 35 34 70 ⓛ 09.00–12.00, 14.00–18.00 Mon–Fri, 14.00–18.00 Sat & Sun ⓝ Bus: A, F, I, T

◢ *Basilique Saint-Rémi*

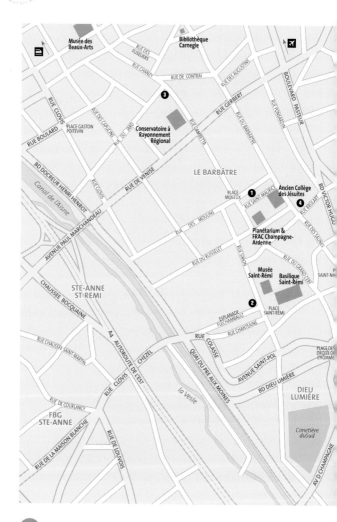

Musée des Beaux-Arts

Bibliothèque Carnegie

RUE DES FUSELIERS

RUE CHANZY

RUE DE CONTRAI

RUE DES AUGUSTINS

BOULEVARD PASTEUR

RUE CLOVIS

RUE DES CAPUCINS

PLACE GASTON POITEVIN

RUE DU JARD

RUE BOULARD

❸

Conservatoire à Rayonnement Régional

RUE GAMBETTA

RUE GERBERT

RUE DU BARBÂTRE

RUE PONSARDIN

BD DOCTEUR HENRI HENROT

RUE DE VENISE

LE BARBÂTRE

Canal de l'Aisne

RUE CLOVIS

❶ PLACE MUSEUX

RUE SAINT-MAURICE

Ancien Collège des Jésuites ❹

BD VICTOR HUGO

RUE BRULART

RUE DES SALINES

AVENUE PAUL MARCHANDEAU

RUE DES MOULINS

Planétarium & FRAC Champagne-Ardenne

RUE SIMON

RUE DU PUISSELET

RUE DU GRAND CERF

SAINT-NI

CHAUSSÉE BOCQUAINE

STE-ANNE ST-REMI

Musée Saint-Rémi

Basilique Saint-Rémi

❷ ESPLANADE FLÉCHAMBAULT

PLACE SAINT-RÉMI

PLACE DES DROGS DE L'HOMME

A4 AUTOROUTE DE L'EST

RUE CHAUSSÉE SAINT-MARTIN

CHEZEL

RUE COLASSE

RUE CHANTEAINE

RUE CLOVIS

QUAI DU PRÉ AUX MOINES

AVENUE SAINT-POL

BD DIEU LUMIÈRE

DIEU LUMIÈRE

FBG STE-ANNE

RUE DE COURLANCY

la Vesle

Cimetière du Sud

RUE DE LA MAISON BLANCHE

RUE DE LOUVOIS

AV D CHAMPAGNE

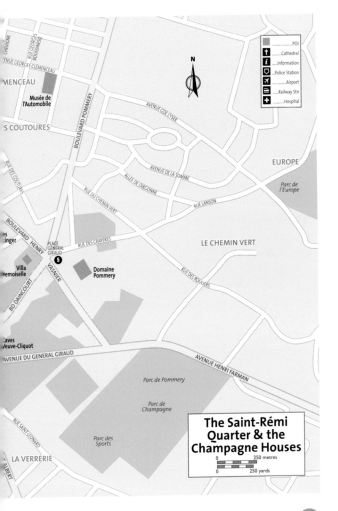

The Saint-Rémi
Quarter & the
Champagne Houses

| 0 | | | 250 metres |
| 0 | | | 250 yards |

Basilique Saint-Rémi

If the cathedral is all about Gothic spikiness and decoration, then the earlier abbey church of Saint-Rémi, built in the 11th century to house the saint's relics, is perhaps equally beautiful but quite different in feel. The sobriety of the Romanesque façade and the long nave with its three tiers of arches give an impression of great length and openness. The east end is in early Gothic style, with a baroque choir that encloses the tomb of Saint Rémi, an elaborate white stone and pink marble confection ringed by statues of Rémi, Clovis and the 12 peers who attended the coronation. Note the rare 12th-century stained glass as well as some modern windows ⓐ Pl. Saint-Rémi ⓛ 08.00–dusk (19.00 at the latest) Bus: A, F, H

Caves Taittinger

Although the building is nondescript from the exterior, its two tiers of cellars are stunning: first, the vaulted Gothic cellars of the medieval abbey of St-Niçaise and beneath them a series of chilly pyramidal chalk Roman quarries. ⓐ 9 pl. Saint-Niçaise ⓣ 03 26 85 84 33 ⓦ www.taittinger.fr ⓛ 09.30–12.00, 14.00–16.30 mid-Mar–mid-Nov; 09.30–12.00, 14.00–16.30 Mon–Fri, mid-Nov–mid-Mar ⓝ Bus: A, Citadine 1 & 2. Admission charge

Caves Veuve-Cliquot

These are the cellars associated with wily widow Barbe Nicole Ponsardin, who directed the Champagne house after the death of her husband. ⓐ 1 pl. des Droits de l'Homme ⓣ 03 26 89 53 90 ⓦ www.veuve-cliquot.fr ⓛ By appointment Mon–Sat, Apr–Oct; Mon–Fri, Nov–Mar. ⓝ Bus: F. Admission charge

HOLY OIL

Reims' destiny was made on 25 December 496 with the baptism in the cathedral of Clovis, the first Merovingian king, by Bishop Rémi in a mass ceremony, alongside 3,000 of his warriors. On the day, however, things didn't start too smoothly, when the christening oil was held up in a traffic jam. Miraculously, a white dove flew down from heaven bearing an ampoule of holy oil. By the ninth century, Archbishop Hincmar had incorporated holy oil – from the sacred ampoule preciously preserved alongside the saint's relics in the Abbey of Saint-Rémi – as part of the coronation ceremony, giving the French monarch semi-sacred status and believed to endow him with healing powers. The ampoule was destroyed in the French Revolution, although a tiny amount of the lotion was saved and used for the coronation of restoration monarch Charles X.

Domaine Pommery

After having studied in England in the early 1800s, Louise Pommery built her Champagne house in a neo-Elizabethan style with a crenellated gateway that resembles Hampton Court. An astute businesswoman, she instituted public visits to the cellars and also commissioned the striking bas reliefs illustrating different aspects of winemaking. A long staircase descends 30 m (98 feet) underground to where some 18 km (11 miles) of tunnels link a series of astonishing Roman chalk quarries. Pommery stands out from the other Champagne houses by combining traditional production with an adventurous contemporary art exhibition in the cellars each summer, so don't be surprised to find videos, sound works and bizarre installations on your route – in 2008, one included zebra finches who nested and strummed Fender guitars. As well as the conventional tour, it is possible to do a tour focused on the artworks. ⓐ 5 pl. du Général Giraud ⓣ 03 26 61 62 56 ⓦ www.pommery.com ⓛ 09.30–19.00 Apr–mid-Nov; 09.30–18.30 mid-Nov–Mar ⓝ Bus: E, V. Admission charge ⓘ Reservation recommended at weekends

Parc de Champagne

The former Parc de Pommery was laid out by the Marquis de Polignac in a sort of early 20th-century health exercise, with all sorts of athletics facilities and idyllic rustic cottages. Replanted with leafy lawns, children's playground and municipal football pitches, it is used for showjumping competitions and a giant picnic concert during the Flâneries Musicales (see page 11). ⓐ 10 av. du Général Giraud ⓣ 03 26 35 52 20 ⓛ 13.00–19.30 Mon, Tues, Thur & Fri, 10.00–19.30 Wed, Sat & Sun, Apr, May, Sept & Oct; 10.00–20.00 June–Aug; 13.00–17.00 Wed, Sat & Sun, Nov & Dec ⓝ Bus: V

Villa Demoiselle

This art nouveau house was commissioned in 1906 by Pommery director Henry Vasnier, according to the principal of 'decoration everywhere'. New owners, the Vrankens, have restored or rather recreated the interiors in a labour of love, using craftsmen to make wooden panelling, tiles, wallpapers, brass light fittings and stained glass for the striking hallway and reception rooms,

● *Domaine Pommery for fine champagne and adventurous art*

furnishing them with a superb collection of art nouveau furniture. This includes some of the original furnishings, an ornate wooden fireplace carved with ombellifers exhibited at the Great Exhibition of 1900, and a drawing room suite by Majorelle. The visit includes a tasting of Demoiselle Champagne. 🄰 Pl. du Général Giraud ☏ 03 26 61 62 56 🕒 By reservation Wed–Sun 🄽 Bus: E, V. Admission charge

CULTURE

Conservatoire à Rayonnement Régional
The curved façade of the vast music and dance school, designed in the 1990s, was apparently inspired by the violin. As well as classrooms, it contains two auditoria. 🄰 20 rue Gambetta ☏ 03 26 86 77 00 🅦 www.crr-reims.fr 🕒 Concert times vary 🄽 Bus: A, F, G, I, T

FRAC Champagne-Ardenne
The regional contemporary art collection puts on exhibitions, commissions artworks, and organises shows and residencies across the region. 🄰 Ancien Collège des Jésuites, 1 pl. Museux ☏ 03 26 05 78 32 🅦 www.frac-champagneardenne.org 🕒 14.00–18.00 Tues–Sat during exhibitions only 🄽 Bus: A, F, I, T

Musée de l'Automobile
Vintage automobiles and fire engines, rare prototypes, motorbikes and bicycles are complemented by a huge collection of pedal cars and toy cars. 🄰 84 av. Georges Clemenceau ☏ 03 26 82 83 84 🅦 www.musee-automobile-reims-champagne.com 🕒 10.00–12.00,

14.00–18.00 Wed–Mon, Apr–Oct; 10.00–12.00, 14.00–17.00 Wed–Mon, Nov–Mar ⊘ Bus: D. Admission charge

Musée Saint-Rémi

Now a museum devoted to the archaeology and history of Reims, its 17th- and 18th-century golden stone architecture reflects the prestige and royal patronage of the Abbaye Saint-Rémi, founded in the seventh century around the tomb of Saint Rémi. Only the impressive 12th-century vaulted chapter house,

⬧ *An old abbey is now the Musée Saint-Rémi*

now containing religious paintings and a sumptuous reliquary that once held the bones of Saint Rémi, remains from earlier medieval buildings. Downstairs the former refectory contains Gallo-Roman funerary statues, mosaics and the marble tomb of Jovin, a Roman general born in Reims, sculpted with a hunting scene with figures, horses, lion and wild boar. Upstairs, reached by a magnificent double staircase, the main treasure is the 16th-century tapestry cycle recounting the life of Saint Rémi in lively strip-cartoon style with text bubbles and multiple episodes from the saint's birth to death via the great fire of Reims and baptism of Clovis. There are also displays of Bronze Age remains, Merovingian tombs, medieval architectural fragments, religious sculpture and military history. ⓐ 53 rue Simon ⓣ 03 26 85 23 36 ⓛ 14.30–18.30 Mon–Fri, 14.00–19.00 Sat & Sun ⓝ Bus: A, F, R, V, Citadine 1 & 2. Admission charge

Planétarium

Star-gazing sessions (in French) in a domed auditorium, plus an elaborate astronomical clock. ⓐ Ancien Collège des Jésuites, 1 pl. Museux ⓣ 03 26 35 34 70 ⓛ 14.45, 15.30, 16.45 Sat & Sun, daily in school hols ⓝ Bus: A, F, I, T. Admission charge

RETAIL THERAPY

Chocolaterie Lothaire An enthusiastic chocolate-maker where you can buy beautifully packaged boxes of chocolates, chocolate Champagne bottles, and special no-sugar chocolate. ⓐ 30 Esplanade Fléchambault ⓣ 03 26 85 54 69 ⓦ www.chocolaterie-lothaire.fr ⓛ 09.00–12.00, 14.00–18.00 Tues–Sat ⓝ Bus: A, F, H, Citadine 1 & 2

Underground This independent record store is the place to discover the native indie scene, as well as imports, old and new vinyl and CDs, flyers and fanzines. ⓐ 44 rue Gambetta ⓣ 03 26 24 19 68 ⓛ 14.00–19.00 Mon, 10.00–12.00, 14.00–19.00 Tues–Sat ⓝ Bus: A, F, G, H, T

TAKING A BREAK

Brasserie Saint-Maurice £ ❶ A pleasant local café with pavement tables on quiet place Museux overlooking the Collège des Jésuites and the Friday afternoon organic food market. ⓐ 38 rue Saint-Maurice ⓣ 03 26 85 45 51 ⓦ www.brasserie-saint-maurice.com ⓛ 07.30–20.30 Mon–Fri, 09.00–13.00 Sat ⓝ Bus: A, F, I, T

Le Fléchambault ❷ A practical café-brasserie just opposite the Basilique Saint-Rémi. ⓐ 2 Esplanade Fléchambault ⓣ 03 26 85 47 11 ⓛ 07.30–20.30 ⓝ Bus: A, F, H, Citadine 1 & 2

AFTER DARK

RESTAURANTS
La Table Anna £ ❸ A cheerful bistro adorned with artworks and knick-knacks. The emphasis is on hearty portions of meat, preferably served with *pommes Anna* (a crunchy buttery cake of thinly sliced potatoes), and traditional homemade desserts. ⓐ 6 rue Gambetta ⓣ 03 26 89 12 12 ⓦ www.latableanna.com ⓛ 12.00–14.30, 19.00–22.30 Tues–Sat, 12.00–14.30 Sun ⓝ Bus: A, F, G, H, T

⬤ *Enjoy a luxurious dining experience (or stay) at Château Les Crayères*

Les Charmes ££ ❹ This intimate restaurant revisits French regional cooking in dishes like beef in wine sauce and cod with preserved lemons. Don't miss the house profiteroles to finish. Bargain menu at lunch time. ⓐ 11 rue Brûlart ☏ 03 26 85 37 63 ⓦ www.restaurantlescharmes.fr ⏰ 12.00–13.15 Mon, 12.00–13.15, 19.30–21.15 Tues–Fri, 19.30–21.15 Sat ⓝ Bus: Citadine

Château Les Crayères £££ ❺ Sumptuous panelled dining room overlooking lovely gardens that's the place for a splurge-of-a-lifetime experience. Chef Didier Elena, who previously headed Alain Ducasse's restaurant in New York, updates haute cuisine, privileging flavour and seasonal ingredients, from an astonishing appetiser of foie gras, sea urchin and diced onion and apple to frogs' legs presented three ways, variations of Bresse hen and a refined remake of bouillabaisse. Perfect service. ⓐ 64 blvd Henry Vasnier ☏ 03 26 82 80 80 ⓦ www.lescrayeres.com ⏰ 12.00–13.45, 19.15–21.30 Wed–Sun, Feb–Dec ⓝ Bus: V

The Promenades & Outer Reims

The grassy Promenades form a natural dividing line between the city centre and the train station and the more recent sprawl beyond, a boundary continued to the west by the River Vesle, Canal de l'Aisne and a noisy motorway (an unfortunate piece of 1970s urban planning that will hopefully soon be diverted to the outskirts). Unlike many French city areas, outer Reims is largely low-rise, with plenty of green spaces, garden cities (such as the Alsatian-style Cité-Jardin du Chemin Vert that marked the social philanthropy of the 1930s reconstruction), a teaching hospital, medical and arts faculties, Reims' management school and some of the city's most active cultural venues.

SIGHTS & ATTRACTIONS

Champagne Mumm

After an introductory film about the vineyards and blending process, the informative tour leads through the long 19th-century cellars of the third biggest producer, where thousands of bottles stand in wooden racks undergoing the painstaking process of riddling. The tour includes a glimpse of the 'wine library', where the oldest bottles go back to the 1890s, and Mumm's underground museum of antique barrel-making, bottling and labelling equipment. Visits finish with a tasting of Cordon Rouge. ❸ 29–34 rue du Champ de Mars ❶ 03 26 49 59 70 Ⓦ www.mumm.com ❶ 09.00–11.00, 14.00–17.00 Mar–Oct; by appointment Mon–Sat, Nov–Feb Ⓝ Bus: K. Admission charge

Chapelle Foujita

The Japanese Ecole de Paris painter Leonard Foujita is best known for his languid portraits painted in Montparnasse in the 1920s and 30s. Following a spiritual experience in the Basilique Saint-Rémi in 1959, he converted to Christianity and, sponsored by René Lalou, director of Mumm, designed this tiny Romanesque-style chapel dedicated to peace, covering the entire interior with delicate sky blue and beige frescoes of Biblical scenes. Grim skulls on the stained glass windows refer to the bombing of Hiroshima and Nagasaki. ⓐ 33 rue du Champ de Mars ⓣ 03 26 40 06 96 ⓛ 14.00–18.00 Thur–Tues, May–Oct ⓝ Bus: K. Admission charge

● *Part of the colourful mosaic façade at Champagne Mumm*

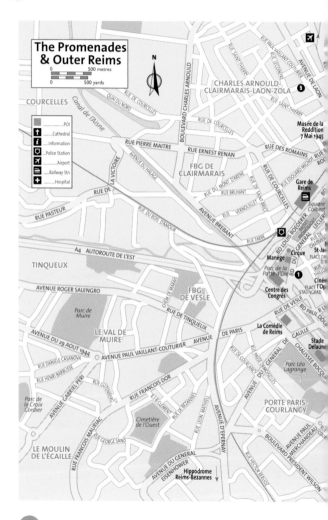

The Promenades & Outer Reims

> **GREEN CHANNEL**
> The inhabitants of Reims are at last rediscovering their
> canal, which was built by Napoleon in the 19th century
> to connect the River Aisne to the River Marne alongside
> the unnavigable River Vesle. Long used only by joggers
> and fishermen, the old towpath has been relandscaped to
> create the Coulée Verte, a 12 km (6 mile) footpath and cycle
> track running right through the heart of the city, between
> Pont du Vrilly in the northwest and Pont de la Neuvillette
> in the southeast.

Cimetière du Nord

This slightly dilapidated cemetery that was laid out in the 1780s
has plenty of romantic sculptures and tombs of Champagne
barons, including the neo-Gothic mausoleum of Cliquot-Ponsardin,
deceased husband of La Veuve Cliquot. ⓐ 1 bis rue du Champ
de Mars ⓣ 03 26 47 26 81 ⓦ http://cimetiere.du.nord.free.fr
ⓛ 08.00–18.30 Apr–Oct; 08.00–19.30 Nov–Mar ⓝ Bus: A, C, F, K

Porte de Mars

The most substantial remnant of Ancient Roman Durocortorum
is this late third-century triumphal arch built in honour of
Emperor Augustus as one of four entrances to the city and
later incorporated within the medieval city wall. Now marooned
on a roundabout, the decoration has been heavily eroded, but
you can see traces of fluted columns and roundels with
portrait busts. ⓐ Pl. de la République ⓝ Bus: A, C, F, K

The Promenades

The long, tree-lined grassy alleys were laid out in the 18th century to form a green band around the city centre. In the middle, Square Colbert is a small flowery garden around a bronze statue of Jean-Baptiste Colbert, Louis XIV's finance minister. In the Hautes Promenades, a memorial to the World War II resistance lines up with the World War I war memorial that was inaugurated in 1930s across place de la République. On the Basses Promenades admire the wrought-iron gateway made for the coronation of Louis XVI, and the red brick and stone Cirque and Manège buildings (see page 100). Beyond here the Parc de la Patte d'Oie was created in 1727. It contains pretty streams, duck ponds and fountains leading to the modern glass façade of the Centre des Congrès.

◯ *The ancient Roman Porte de Mars*

CULTURE

La Cartonnerie

Opened in 2005, this venue has transformed Reims' live music scene with its programme of French indie groups, reggae, new *chanson* and big names of electronic music (Air and Tricky, for instance, in 2008). As well as two concert halls, there are rehearsal studios, a library, exhibition space and a bar decorated by artists and designers. ⓐ 84 rue du Dr Lemoine ⓣ 03 26 82 72 45 or 03 26 36 72 40 ⓦ www.cartonnerie.fr ⓒ Times vary according to what's on ⓝ Bus: F & K

Le Cirque/Le Manège de Reims

The lovely red brick and stone polygonal circus building and its *manège* (originally a riding school and gymnasium) have been beautifully restored and are now one of the most dynamic cultural centres in Reims, with a programme dedicated to all forms of contemporary dance, urban dance and circus, along with art shows and cine-concerts. ⓐ 2 blvd du Général Leclerc ⓣ 03 26 47 30 40 ⓦ www.manegedereims.com ⓒ Shows: times vary according to what's on; exhibitions: 14.00–19.00 ⓝ Bus: Citadine 1 & 2

La Comédie de Reims

This modern theatre is home to the Centre Dramatique National (National Drama Centre), which is highly reputed for its adventurous programming including the premieres of numerous new works, both its own productions and visiting productions by renowned directors. ⓐ 3 Chaussée Bocquaine

☎ 03 26 48 49 00 **Ⓦ** www.lacomediedereims.fr **🕐** Times vary according to what's on **Ⓝ** Bus: B, K, M, N

Musée de la Reddition 7 mai 1945

This fascinating museum reminds the visitor that the end of World War II was signed on this very spot on 7 May 1945 in the

🔺 *Visit Le Manège de Reims for a variety of performance arts*

red brick *lycée* where General Dwight Eisenhower had installed his operations HQ after the liberation of Reims in 1944. (The official VE date of 8 May is when the news appeared in the press and a second signature was made in Berlin in the Russian presence.) Rare archive film footage shows the arrival of German General Jodl and the signature of surrender. The heart of the display is the extraordinarily atmospheric room where the signature actually took place, now viewed behind a glass screen, and preserved as it was at the time, with its massive table surrounded by chairs and walls covered in maps of Europe, showing Allied offensives and resources. ⓐ 12 rue Franklin Roosevelt ⓣ 03 26 47 84 19 ⓛ 10.00–12.00, 14.00–18.00 Wed–Mon ⓝ Bus: A, C, F. Admission charge

RETAIL THERAPY

Galerie Jamin Half a dozen antiques dealers selling period furniture, art deco lamps, *objets d'art* and antiquarian books. ⓐ 6 blvd Jamin ⓣ 03 26 07 12 27 ⓦ www.galeriejamin.com ⓛ 10.00–19.00 Sat & Sun, 14.00–18.00 Mon ⓝ Bus: B

TAKING A BREAK

Le Seven Café £ ❶ A friendly, funky bar just opposite the Centre des Congrès, with metal Chinese dragons snaking over the bar. Champagne by the glass and lasagne, salads and omelettes are served all day. ⓐ 79 blvd du Général Leclerc ⓒ 03 26 47 83 33 ⓛ 08.00–01.30 Mon–Sat (also some Sun) ⓝ Bus: B, K, M, N

Le Verre des Anges £ ❷ At this small wine shop and bar, you can sample unusual regional wines accompanied by *charcuterie*, cheeses and some surprisingly ambitious hot dishes of the day. ⓐ 10 av. Jean Jaurès ❶ 03 26 04 50 69 ⓛ 10.00–19.00 Mon–Wed & Sat, 10.00–00.00 Thur & Fri ⓝ Bus: B

AFTER DARK

RESTAURANTS

Le Jamin £ ❸ Classic French cuisine – foie gras, terrines, fish in *beurre blanc* sauces – served in quite a formal setting. ⓐ 18 blvd Jamin ❶ 03 26 07 37 30 ⓦ www.lejamin.com ⓛ 12.00–14.00, 19.30–22.00 Tues–Sat, 12.00–14.00 Sun ⓝ Bus: B

Les Sarments £ ❹ In a rustic interior totally dedicated to the grape, this convivial bistro serves up traditional regional cooking and homemade foie gras. ⓐ 48 rue Léon Faucher 5 ❶ 03 26 07 43 33 ⓦ www.lessarmentsreims.fr ⓛ 12.00–14.00, 18.00–22.00 Tues–Sat, 12.00–14.00 Sun ⓝ Bus: K

L'Assiette Champenoise £££ ❺ Arnaud Lallement is one of the bright young talents of French cuisine. After taking over the swish family auberge on the edge of town, he now presents inventive modern cooking based around grand ingredients, such as ceps, langoustines, lamb and pigeon, each cooked in multiple ways. Reserve ahead. ⓐ 40 rue Paul Vaillant Couturier, Tinqueux ❶ 03 26 84 64 64 ⓦ www.assiettechampenoise.com ⓛ 19.30–21.30 Wed, 12.00–14.00, 19.30–21.30 Thur–Mon ⓝ Bus: B

BARS & CLUBS

L'Appart Café With its riveted metal bar and steel bar stools, this relaxed, grungy café is making its mark with its laid-back mood and live music programming that goes from electro DJs to reggae or Arabo-Israeli klezmer. ⓐ 9 av. de Laon ⓣ 03 26 47 51 40 ⓦ www.lappartcafe.com ⓛ 17.00–00.30 Tues–Thur, 17.00–01.30 Fri & Sat ⓝ Bus: A, C, F

Factory This longstanding feature of Reims' nightlife draws a slightly older 30-something crowd, who like the civilised cocktail bar ambience. On Thursdays, there's a popular 'after work' event with lounge music and a buffet, before the club gets going to groove, house and disco. ⓐ 87 av. de Paris ⓣ 03 26 83 09 26 ⓦ www.factorylounge.com ⓛ 19.00–03.30 Thur, 23.00–04.30 Fri, Sat & eve of public holidays ⓝ Bus: B. Admission charge Sat

Guest Club Trendy club that's small and selective, drawing a young, pretty set. On Thursday it's 90s revival (already). ⓐ 18 av. de Paris ⓣ 03 26 84 05 31 ⓦ www.guestclub.fr ⓛ 23.30–05.00 Thur–Sat & eve of public holidays

Pop Art Café An arty all-rounder with DJs, live music, exhibitions, slam poetry and improvised *soirées*. Unpretentious and packed with students. ⓐ 103 rue de Neufchatel, north of rue Emile Zola ⓣ 03 26 04 87 93 ⓦ www.popartcafe.fr ⓛ 19.00–00.30 Mon–Thur, 19.00–01.30 Fri & Sat ⓝ Bus: C

ⓞ *Under the arches in place Ducale at Charleville-Mézières*

Epernay & the Champagne Route

Just 30 km (19 miles) south of Reims, Epernay rivals it for the title of Champagne-producing capital. Lying between the two, the Montagne de Reims is a regional nature park, with pretty villages and vines (especially powerful Pinot Noir) covering the lower slopes and wooded hilltops above. The wine route continues west of Epernay along the Marne valley, domain of Pinot Meunier, to Dormans, and southwards towards Sézanne through the slopes of the Côte des Blancs, which are devoted to the white Chardonnay grape. There are plenty of opportunities for visiting vineyards and for country walks. It's a good idea to pick up the *La Marne Champagne Discovery Guide* (W www.tourisme-en-champagne.com), published by the Marne tourist board, for information on cellars open for visits.

GETTING THERE

There are several trains a day between the Gare de Reims and Epernay, taking between 20 and 30 minutes, but by far the best way to explore the area is by car. The most direct route is by the N51, which crosses over the centre of the Montagne de Reims. However, if you have the time, it is more rewarding to follow the well-signposted Route de Champagne, which meanders round the eastern slopes along the D26 and D19 through scenic vineyards and attractive Grand Cru villages, such as Rilly-la-Montagne, Verzenay, Bouzy, Ambonnay and Ay, where almost every other home seems to belong to a Champagne producer, before crossing the River Marne to Epernay.

⬥ *The river Marne flows through a valley of Champagne vineyards*

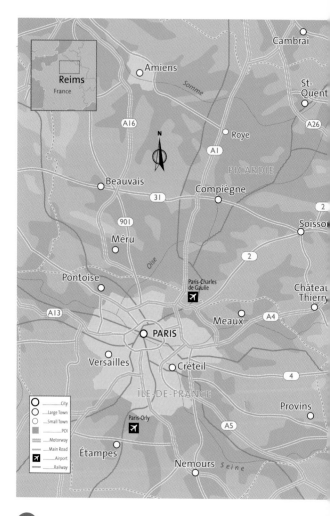

For those without transport, the Office de Tourisme de Reims (see page 136) runs a four-hour bilingual coach tour of the Montagne de Reims wine route on Saturday afternoons in summer, leaving from the cathedral (see page 58) and taking in a visit to a producer (but do reserve in advance).

⬥ Downtown Epernay

SIGHTS & ATTRACTIONS

Avenue de Champagne, Epernay

The Champagne equivalent of Millionaires' Row is also known locally as 'le Faubourg de la Folie' (crazy street). Here the fanciful 19th-century mansions of Epernay's Champagne barons, along with their warehouses and cellars, are lined up side by side in an evocative roll call of names that includes Perrier-Jouët, Moët & Chandon, Esteban, Pol Roger and Mercier. At no. 9, the former mansion of Auban Moët is now the town hall, which sits in a park designed by the Buhler brothers.

Bateau Champagne Vallée

Highly enjoyable 90-minute boat trips on the River Marne on – of all things – a replica of a Mississippi paddle steamer. The organisers also run lunch cruises and evening dinner cruises with cabaret. ⓐ Quai de la Marne, Cumières; offices: 12 rue de la Coopérative, Cumières ⓣ 03 26 54 49 51 ⓦ www.champagne-et-croisiere.com ⓛ Guaranteed sailing 15.30 Tues–Sun, Easter–15 Sept (other times by reservation); by reservation 15 Mar–Easter, 16 Sept–15 Dec

Champagne Castellane

Castellane's gorgeously extravagant concrete and glazed tile tower is an Epernay landmark. Cellar tours incorporate a bracing 237-step climb to the top of the tower and a visit to the museum which outlines the history of winemaking and bottling through models, old equipment and vintage advertising posters. ⓐ 57 rue de Verdun, Epernay ⓣ 03 26 51 19 11 ⓦ www.castellane.com

🕐 10.00–11.15, 14.00–17.15 Mar–Dec; 10.00–11.15, 14.00–17.15 Sat & Sun, Jan & Feb Admission charge

Champagne Leclerc-Briant

Most definitely a place for sporty types and adrenalin junkies: you can abseil 30 m (98 ½ feet) down a hole into the cellars under the watchful eye and tutelage of a qualified potholer at this small Champagne house, which cultivates its wines according to bio-dynamic principles. ⓐ 67 rue Claude Ruelle, Epernay ⓣ 03 26 54 45 33 ⓦ www.leclercbriant.com 🕐 09.00–12.00, 13.30–17.00 Mon–Fri, Sept–July; abseiling visits by reservation. Admission charge

Champagne Mercier

Unlike most of the Champagne houses that play on the beauty and antiquity of their cellars, Mercier emphasises its modernity and the marketing skill of founder Eugène Mercier, whose ingenious publicity stunts included the giant wooden barrel (now visible in the visitor centre) that was towed to Paris by 12 pairs of oxen and 18 horses for the Exposition Universelle in 1889. He also commissioned one of the first ever advertising films (made by the Lumière brothers and screened at the Exposition Universelle of 1900), and took customers up for Champagne tastings in a hot air balloon. After an introductory film, the visit floats you down slowly at balloon speed by glass-sided lift into the cellars and then glides you smoothly through the tunnels in a laser-guided electric train. ⓐ 68 av. de Champagne, Epernay ⓣ 03 26 51 22 22 🕐 09.30–11.30, 14.00–16.30 mid-Mar–mid-Nov; 09.30–11.30,

14.00–16.30 Thur–Mon, mid-Feb–mid-Mar, mid-Nov–mid-Dec.
Admission charge

DUG IN

The Battle of the Marne, which was fought between 5 and
12 September 1914, was considered to be one of the turning
points of World War I. Four thousand French reinforcements
were carried to the front by taxi from Paris, ensuring
German defeat and preventing the invasion of the capital,
but also marking the start of four long and gruelling years
of trench warfare. The nearest reminder of this epoch to
Reims is the atmospheric Fort de la Pompelle, a fortification
tunnelled into a chalk ridge just south of the city, which
formed part of a ring of defences put up in 1880-83 after
the 1870 Franco-Prussian War. Captured by German troops
on 4 September 1914, it was recaptured by the French infantry
on 24 September after the Battle of the Marne and held by
successive regiments, including Russian troops loaned by
the Tsar, during four years of incessant bombardment, mines
and gas attacks. Today part of the living quarters are open
to the public, where tunnels now contain a collection of
cannons and mortar shells, a horse-drawn campaign kitchen,
everyday items and photos from the trenches, and a colossal
array of Prussian helmets and swords. ❷ Route de Chalons-
en-Champagne ☎ 03 26 49 11 85 ⏰ 11.00–18.00 Mon &
Wed–Fri, 11.00–19.00 Sat & Sun, Apr–Oct; 10.00–17.00
Wed–Mon, Nov–Mar. Admission charge

Champagne Moët et Chandon

Descend through two layers of vast cellars, and have a thoroughly good time doing so, in this colossal Champagne house. ❷ 18 av. de Champagne, Epernay ❶ 03 26 51 20 20 ❼ www.moet.com ❶ By reservation: 09.30–11.30, 14.00–16.30 mid-Mar–mid-Nov; 09.30–11.30, 14.00–16.30 Mon–Fri, mid-Nov–mid-Mar. Admission charge

Château de Pierry

This pretty U-shaped château in the start of the Côte des Blancs just south of Epernay was built in the early 18th century by Count Claude Antoine de Choiseul Beaupré, Bishop of Châlons, to serve as his country residence. Now in the tenth-generation hands of the Gobillaud family, you can visit the reception rooms, period apartments, gardens and cellars. The whole experience provides a clear vision of smallscale Champagne production that's quite different from that given by the big Champagne houses. ❷ Pierry ❶ 03 26 54 05 11 ❼ www.château-de-pierry.fr ❶ 09.00–11.00, 14.00–16.30 Mon, Tues & Thur–Sat. Admission charge

Les Faux de Verzy

This ancient forest of twisted beech trees, with their bizarre – and almost grotesque – spiralling branches, is one of the most popular sights in the region. These strange arboreal forms are actually a rare natural phenomenon that's thought to be caused by some sort of genetic mutation. ❷ From Verzy follow signs to Les Faux on Louvois road

CULTURE

Musée de la Vigne

This curious lighthouse standing in a vineyard near the village of Verzenay was constructed as a publicity stunt at the start of the 20th century and originally contained an open air café at the base. After its owners sank into bankruptcy, it was converted into a modern museum that uses multimedia techniques to explain the history and methods of Champagne making. ⓐ Verzenay ① 03 26 07 87 87 ⓦ www.lepharedeverzenay.com ⓒ 10.00–17.00 Tues–Sun, mid-Jan–Dec. Admission charge

TAKING A BREAK

C comme Champagne Both a shop selling Champagnes from a selection of independent producers and a spacious tasting bar where you can try them out. A good place to get beyond the big names and discover some of the interesting smaller labels. ⓐ 8 rue Gambetta, Epernay ① 03 26 32 09 55 ⓦ www.c-comme.fr ⓒ 11.00–20.00

AFTER DARK

RESTAURANTS

L'Auberge Champenoise £ A big rustic restaurant on the start of the Côte des Blancs that's been in the same family for four generations. Sample well-prepared regional recipes, such as snails in Champagne and cream sauce, trout à l'Ardennaise, ice cream soufflé with Reims pink biscuits and strawberries doused in Champagne.

The lovingly composed wine list has over 400 references. There are also 55 simple yet comfortable bedrooms (£). ⓐ Moussy (village des coteaux sud), Épernay ⓣ 03 26 54 03 48 ⓦ www.auberge-champenoise.com ⓛ 12.00–14.00, 19.30–21.30 Tues–Sat, 12.00–14.00 Sun

La Table Kobus ££ The setting suggests belle époque nostalgia, but the creative seasonal market cooking of haute cuisine trained Thierry Siden has a decidedly contemporary form of rustic chic. Located behind the church in Epernay. ⓐ 3 rue du Dr Rousseau, Epernay ⓣ 03 26 51 53 53 ⓦ www.latablekobus.com ⓛ 12.00–14.00, 19.30–21.15 Tues, Wed, Fri & Sat, 12.00–14.00 Thur & Sun

BARS & CLUBS
Le Vintage Café A sultry Champagne bar with clubby atmosphere; just to shake things up a bit, there are house and electro DJs at weekends. ⓐ 34 rue du Dr Verron, Epernay ⓣ No phone ⓦ www.myspace.com/vintage_epernay ⓛ Evenings Tues–Sun

ACCOMMODATION

La Cloche £ Rooms are simple and bathrooms tiny, but this cheerful hotel and restaurant is a popular budget option in the centre of Epernay. ⓐ 3–5 pl. Mendès France, Epernay ⓣ 03 26 55 15 15 ⓦ www.hotel-la-cloche.com

Château d'Etoges ££–£££ Louis XIV and Louis XVI were both guests at this gorgeous 17th-century château, where you can still row around the moat. Comfortable rooms, some with romantic canopies, and a restaurant serving good, classic cuisine. ⓐ 4 rue Richebourg, Etoges ⓣ 03 26 59 30 08 ⓦ www.chateau-etoges.com

Villa Eugène ££–£££ A lovely boutique hotel in a house built by Eugène Mercier that's been decorated with lashings of taste. The 15 romantic bedrooms come in either Louis XVI or colonial style and there's a conservatory overlooking the garden for breakfast. Reserve well ahead, especially for weekends. ⓐ 82–84 av. de Champagne, Epernay ⓣ 03 26 32 44 76

⬤ *Row around the moat at romantic Château d'Etoges*

Into the Ardennes

A trip to the Ardennes region towards the Belgian border gives a taste of provincial France that feels a world apart from Reims. The Meuse river meanders in sometimes spectacular loops at the foot of the wooded Ardennes uplands and, although there's nothing dramatic about these mountains, there is still an impression of savage nature here – the symbol of the Ardennes is the *sanglier* (or wild boar) and winter game will frequently crop up on restaurant menus. The two main towns are the regional capital Charleville-Mézières and the former royal textile town of Sedan, home to the largest fortress in Europe. If you're looking for somewhere to stay, Sedan makes a particularly agreeable base, with its well-restored historic centre and a couple of pleasant hotels. A reminder of this area's proximity to Belgium is that here you are in beer country, a tradition that has recently been revived – look out for the artisanal Princesse beer that's made in Sedan.

GETTING THERE

Charleville-Mézières (60 minutes) and Sedan (75 minutes) are served by several trains a day from the Gare de Reims. To explore the Meuse valley and the Ardennes hills, however, it is easiest to go by car. Charleville-Mézières is 86 km (53 miles) from Reims by the N51 and A34. From Charleville-Mézieres, take the D764 or A203 east to Sedan or the D1 west along the Meuse to Monthermé and Revin.

◆ *Pavilion in place Ducale, Charleville-Mézières*

SIGHTS & ATTRACTIONS

Charleville-Mézières

Until 1966, this was two separate towns: medieval Mézières and the 17th-century city of Charleville. Mézières still has some of its sturdy fortifications jutting into the river, as well as the imposing Basilique Notre-Dame d'Espérance, a large Gothic church that is especially notable for its modern stained glass designed in the 1950s by René Durrbach, evoking Biblical themes with swirly geometric forms. Across the river, Charleville was founded in the early 17th century by Charles de Gonzague, Duke of Nevers and Rethel and a descendent of the Dukes of Mantua, who laid the city out on a grid plan around the magnificent ducal square and named it after himself. The birthplace of Arthur Rimbaud (see page 124), Charleville-Mézières is also known for its international puppet festival and in fact has a puppetry school on place Winston Churchill. A giant automaton, the Grand Marionnettiste, animates a clock on the school's façade.

Historium du Château Fort

Europe's largest fortress was begun in 1424 by Evrard, Comte de Marck, and continued by the Princes de Marck and the Tour d'Auvergne family in the 16th century, when Sedan was an independent principality. Its surrender after a siege during the 1870 Franco-Prussian War marked Napoleon III's defeat and the end of the Second Empire. During World War I it was used as an internment camp for French and Belgian resistants. The castle is not for the infirm, with lots of dank, drippy tunnels and steep stairways constructed within the massive castle walls. The route

takes in various garrison rooms, where some uncommonly realistic wax figures are used discreetly and to good effect to give a picture of the castle's military functioning, the rampart walk with cannons, the Galerie des Princes, hung with portraits and tapestries, plus adjoining rooms with displays of ceramics and furniture, and the Salle des Gardes, which has an impressive circular wooden vault.
ⓐ Sedan ⓣ 03 24 29 98 80 ⓛ 10.00–12.00, 13.30–17.00 Apr–June & winter school hols; 10.00–18.00 July & Aug; 10.00–12.00, 13.30–16.00 Sat & Sun, Sept–Mar. Admission charge

Monthermé
A picturesque small town occupying a loop in the Meuse, with views of wooded hillsides and plenty of footpaths leading up to a cluster of rocks with poetic names.

Place Ducale, Charleville-Mézières
It's worth the trip to Charleville just to see this grand arcaded square, designed by Clément Métézeau in around 1608, and considered the big cousin of the beautiful but smaller Place des Vosges in Paris, which was possibly also designed by Métézeau or by his brother, Louis. The 24 pavilions have a distinctly Flemish touch with their red brick, stone arcades and steeply pitched roofs of Ardennes slate. Needless to say, the square itself has become a car park, but there are several cafés and bistros under the arcades, as well as the well-presented Musée de l'Ardenne (see page 123).

Revin
This old iron-working town has a spectacular setting in a double meander of the Meuse. The half-timbered 'Spanish house', dating

● *Château Fort in Sedan*

from the period when Revin was actually part of Spanish-ruled Flanders, contains the **Musée du Vieux Revin** (ⓐ 2 rue Victor Hugo ⓣ 03 24 40 34 91), a small and informative museum of local history and folk art.

Sedan

Most people come to Sedan to visit its vast Château Fort (see page 120) but the town has a lively, well-restored historic centre reflecting its past as an intellectual centre during the Wars of Religion and, later, as a wealthy textile and metal-working town. Notable buildings include the 17th-century Château Bas just beneath the fortress, fine 18th-century drapers' houses and workshops, the Dijonval (a former royal sheet factory) and the imposing Eglise Saint-Charles, with its baroque choir and twin slate towers.

CULTURE

Musée de l'Ardenne

Housed in a series of historic buildings and a modern glass extension, this award-winning museum presents Roman and Merovingian pottery and jewellery and other archaeological finds, firearms made in the town and the Ardennes' traditional trades of wood-, iron- and slate-working. It also gives a view of the workings of the Grand Marionnettiste automaton on place Winston Churchill. ⓐ 31 pl. Ducale, Charleville-Mézières ⓣ 03 24 32 44 60 ⓦ www.charleville-mezieres.org ⓛ 10.00–12.00, 14.00–18.00 Tues–Sun. Admission charge

POETIC PASSION

Fuelling the image of absinthe and tortured, long-haired bohemian poets, the torrid love affair between Arthur Rimbaud, Charleville-Mézières's most famous son, and Paul Verlaine came to an end – perhaps unsurprisingly – when the latter wounded the former with a revolver in 1873; but it has continued to inspire artists and rock stars ever since. A prodigious talent, Rimbaud wrote most of his poetry as a teenager in Charleville-Mézières, giving up composition in his 20s to wander the globe before dying of cancer in Marseille at the age of 37 and being buried in Charleville cemetery. Verlaine too is associated with the area, writing his long poem Sagesse in the Auberge du Lion d'Or in Juniville, now the Musée Verlaine.

Musée Rimbaud/Maison d'Ailleurs

The former ducal watermill, which spans a branch of the Meuse to a pretty island park, is now a museum dedicated to the town's most famous son. The collection includes personal souvenirs, some original manuscripts, photos, drawings and a copy of Fantin-Latour's famous painting *Un Coin de Table*, now in the Musée d'Orsay, depicting Rimbaud, Verlaine and other literary figures. Across the street, the Maison d'Ailleurs, the house where Rimbaud lived as a teenager and wrote much of his poetry, has been left unfurnished and uses atmospheric sound and video projections to evoke the poet's life and his travels to London, Brussels and Africa.
ⓐ Quai Arthur Rimbaud, Charleville-Mézières ⓣ 03 24 32 44 65

ⓦ www.charleville-mezieres.org ⓛ 10.00–12.00, 14.00–18.00 Tues–Sun. Admission charge

AFTER DARK

HOTELS & RESTAURANTS

A L'Instant T £ Designer style has arrived in Sedan with this striking restaurant and lounge bar. Brunch on Sunday. ⓐ 7 promenade des Pêcheurs, Sedan ⓣ 03 24 33 10 09 ⓦ www.alinstantt.com ⓛ Bar: 09.00–22.30; meals served: 12.00–14.30, 19.00–21.30

La Côte à l'Os ££ This brasserie has been serving up shellfish on the one hand and steaks and local game on the other for over 20 years. ⓐ 11 cours Aristide Briand, Charleville-Mézières ⓣ 03 24 59 20 16 ⓦ www.restaurant-charleville-lacotealos.fr ⓛ 12.00–14.00, 19.00–23.00 Mon–Sat, 12.00–14.00 Sun

⬥ *A L'Instant T is a relaxing place to dine*

Hôtel Le Château Fort ££ A gorgeous place to stay within the Sedan fortress itself, given a touch of contemporary chic in elegant bedrooms, some of them spacious duplexes with modern bathrooms. There's a long salon with leather club chairs and a little nook carved into the rock. The restaurant Le Tour d'Auvergne (**££**) serves well-presented modern seasonal cooking. ⓐ Porte des Princes, Sedan ⓣ 03 24 26 11 00 ⓦ www.hotelfp-sedan.com

Hôtel Saint-Michel ££ This hotel in an attractive stone house in the old town just beneath the Château Fort has been totally renovated and is now a very comfortable affair, decorated with warm colours and sophisticated lighting. The downstairs restaurant is the place to sample sustaining local specialities, such as wild boar stew. ⓐ 3 rue Saint-Michel, Sedan ⓣ 03 24 29 04 61 ⓦ www.le-saint-michel.fr

BARS
Au Roy de la Bière A Sedan institution with a big choice of French and Belgian beers, including locally made Princesse on tap. ⓐ 19 place de la Halle, Sedan ⓣ 03 24 29 01 74 ⓛ 10.00–02.00 Tues–Sun

● *The unusual setting of the Reims tourist office*

Directory

GETTING THERE

By air

The nearest airport, **Paris Charles de Gaulle**
(ⓦ www.aeroportsdeparis.fr) at Roissy in the Ile-de-France,
is France's biggest airport and is served by international flights
from all over the world. It is 155 km (98 miles) from Reims by car
by the A1, A104 and A4 motorways or by direct high-speed train
link between Aéroport CDG TGV and Champagne-Ardenne TGV
station (a journey time of 30 minutes).

Many people are aware that air travel emits CO_2, which
contributes to climate change. You may be interested in the
possibility of lessening the environmental impact of your flight
through **Climate Care** (ⓦ www.climatecare.org), which offsets
your CO_2 by funding environmental projects around the world.

By rail

Reims is on the high-speed Paris–Strasbourg TGV line, served by
direct trains from Paris Gare de l'Est in just 45 minutes. As well
as the Gare de Reims in the town centre (see page 48), some
trains arrive at the station Champagne-Ardenne constructed in
the countryside 5 km (3 miles) outside Reims (see page 48). Be
sure to *composter* (validate) your ticket in the yellow machines
at the entrance to the platforms before getting on the train.

There are frequent Eurostar trains from London St Pancras
International (and Ebbsfleet and Ashford International) to Paris
Gare du Nord (taking approximately 2 hours, 25 minutes), from
where it is a five-minute walk to Gare de l'Est. It is also possible

to change trains in Lille, where there are three TGVs a day to Gare TGV Champagne-Ardenne (a journey time of approximately 1 hour, 25 minutes).

Eurostar ⓘ UK 08705 186186 ⓦ www.eurostar.com

SNCF ⓘ 3635 or 08 92 35 35 35; regional trains: 08 91 67 10 08 ⓦ www.voyages-sncf.com

The monthly *Thomas Cook European Rail Timetable* has up-to-date schedules for European international and national train services. **Thomas Cook European Rail Timetable** ⓘ UK 01733 416477, USA 1 800 322 3834 ⓦ www.thomascookpublishing.com

🔺 *Art deco window and clock at the Gare de l'Est*

By road

Reims is 145 km (90 miles) from Paris by the A4 motorway, which passes right through the eastern side of town, and 270 km (170 miles) from Calais on the A26. You can bring your car from the UK through the Channel Tunnel with Eurotunnel, or by car ferry from Dover to the ports of Boulogne-sur-Mer, Calais or Dunkerque.

Eurotunnel Channel Tunnel from Folkestone to Calais

ⓘ UK 08705 353535, France 08 10 63 03 04 ⓦ www.eurotunnel.com

Norfolk Line Ferries between Dover and Dunkerque

ⓘ UK 0844 847 5042, France 03 28 59 01 01 ⓦ www.norfolkline.com

P&O Ferries between Dover and Calais ⓘ UK 08716 645645, France 08 25 12 01 56 ⓦ www.poferries.fr

SeaFrance Ferries between Dover and Calais ⓘ UK 08705 711711, France 08 25 08 25 05 ⓦ www.seafrance.com

Speedferries Ferries between Dover and Boulogne-sur-Mer

ⓘ UK 0871 222 7456, from outside UK +44 8702 200 570

Drive on the right in France and overtake on the left. Seatbelts are compulsory for both front and rear seats and children under ten are not allowed to sit in the front. Speed limits are 130 km/h (80 mph) on motorways, 110 km/h (70 mph) on dual carriageways, 90 km/h (55 mph) on other country roads and 50 km/h (30 mph) in urban areas, with 30 km/h (20 mph) in certain designated zones. Speed limits are reduced in wet weather and there are speed radars on some roads. It is obligatory to carry a fluorescent waistcoat and hazard triangle in case of breakdown.

ENTRY FORMALITIES

European Union citizens do not need a visa to visit France but do need a valid identity card or passport. Citizens of the USA,

Canada, Australia and New Zealand do not need a visa for stays of less than 90 days; South African visitors require a visa; visitors from other countries may require a visa and should enquire at the French embassy in their country before travelling. EU citizens may bring in objects for personal consumption, provided they are not banned or have been bought outside the EU.

MONEY

France is part of the euro (€) zone. There are banknotes in €5, €10, €20, €50, €100, €200 and €500 denominations, with coins for 1, 2, 5, 10, 20 and 50 cents and €1 and €2. Try to avoid having large-denomination €200 and €500 notes, which many shops and restaurants are unwilling to accept. Do note that not all banks have change facilities and that traveller's cheques are not widely used; it is usually easiest to take money from ATMs which are plentiful in main towns such as Reims.

Credit cards are widely used in France, especially Visa and MasterCard, although there may be a minimum sum you're required to spend (often around €15).

If your credit card is lost or stolen, call one of the following numbers to *faire opposition* (block your card):

American Express ℹ 01 47 77 72 00
Diners Club ℹ 08 10 31 41 59
Eurocard/MasterCard ℹ 08 00 90 13 87
Groupement des Cartes Bancaires ℹ 08 92 70 57 05
Visa ℹ 08 92 70 57 05

HEALTH, SAFETY & CRIME

There are no special food and drink precautions to take. Tap water is safe to drink in France, unless marked 'eau non potable'. There are no obligatory vaccinations for entry into France.

Healthcare in France is usually of a high standard and Reims has a well-respected university teaching hospital. Pharmacies (indicated by a flashing green cross) are widespread and can usually offer advice and basic first aid. At night and on Sundays, check in pharmacy windows or call ☎ 3237 for the address of the *pharmacie de garde* (duty chemist). Your hotel should be able to recommend a *médecin généraliste* (GP). Outside hours, *SOS Médecins* (see page 138) can answer house calls and offer medical advice by phone (in French).

EU nationals on holiday in France are entitled to use the French Social Security system, which refunds up to 70 per cent of medical expenses; for more information see ⓦ www.nhs.uk/Healthcareabroad. To get a refund, make sure you have a free **EHIC** (European Health Insurance Card ☎ 0845 606 2030 ⓦ www.ehic.org.uk) before leaving the UK. Make sure that the doctor you consult is *conventionné* (registered with the French health service, with approved treatment rates). You will have to pay the doctor or dentist directly, who will issue you with a *feuille de soins*, but you should be able to claim back part of the treatment cost when you are back in the UK. Non-EU nationals should make sure they have travel insurance to cover health care. For emergency numbers and 24-hour casualty services see page 138.

Reims is not generally a dangerous city, although the usual precautions apply about not leaving items visible in the car or walking through parks late at night. Crimes should be reported to the police (see page 138).

OPENING HOURS

Shops in Reims generally open between 09.30 or 10.00 to 12.00 and 14.00 to 19.00 Monday to Saturday; many close on Monday morning and larger stores and supermarkets generally stay open at lunchtime. Some bakers and food shops open on Sunday morning, as do some supermarkets.

Banks usually open from 09.00 to 12.00 and 14.00 to 17.00 Monday to Friday. Some close on Monday and open on Saturday morning instead.

Most museums open from 10.00 to 12.00, then 14.00 to 18.00 (sometimes with longer hours in summer). Many museums close on either Monday or Tuesday.

Restaurants generally serve food from 12.00 to 14.00 and then from 19.30 to 22.00. Some brasseries serve food after midnight; smaller, family-run establishments and owner-chefs may close for all or part of August. Cafés will often serve sandwiches and snacks all day.

TOILETS

There are public toilets near the cathedral and some coin operated 'super-loos' around the town. If using the toilets in a café, it is polite to at least order a coffee at the bar.

CHILDREN

In hotels, children under 12 can often stay for free in their parents' room with a cot or folding bed, or there may be family rooms. Baby food and disposable nappies are available in any supermarket, though breast feeding in public is frowned upon – be discreet. Taking children to restaurants is part of everyday life in France.

Some places propose simple menus, often of the chicken, beefburger, ham and chips and ice cream variety; at other places they may offer to prepare something simple or you can order starters (*charcuterie* or ham and melon are often popular) or share a main course.

Visiting Champagne cellars may not sound an obvious attraction with children but many kids will enjoy the experience of the chilly underground tunnels: try Pommery (see page 85) with its artworks, while the Musée de la Vigne in Verzeney (see page 115) is firmly aimed at families. Children under 16 get in free to municipal museums; under 18s to national museums. Other good sightseeing options include the huge castle in Sedan, where waxworks give a vivid picture of the functioning of a military fortress.

Small children enjoy the ducks in Parc de la Patte d'Oie and the playgrounds of Parc Léo Legrange. There's a pretty vintage merry-go-round on rue Condorcet behind the Eglise Saint-Jacques (see page 63). The swimming pool and ice rink at Chaussée Bocquaine (see page 35) are very popular with kids; there are special skating sessions for children on Sunday mornings. Méli'môme (see page 10) is a festival of theatre, dance and music for toddlers and children each spring.

COMMUNICATIONS
Internet
Wi-Fi access is available in many hotels and some cafés. One particularly reliable venue is:
Clique et Croque A spacious, central internet café with plenty of computers, Wi-Fi area, cybergames, photocopying and snacks.

TELEPHONING FRANCE

To dial Reims from abroad, dial the French country code +33 and leave off the zero at the start of the ten-digit number.

TELEPHONING ABROAD

To dial abroad from France, dial 00, followed by the country code and then the number. Country codes from France: UK 44; Republic of Ireland 353; USA and Canada 1; Australia 61; New Zealand 64; South Africa 27.

ⓐ 19 rue Chanzy ⓣ 03 26 86 93 92 ⓦ www.cliqueetcroque.com
ⓛ 10.00–00.00 Mon–Sat, 14.00–20.00 Sun

Phone

All phone numbers in France have ten digits. Numbers in Reims and the rest of northeastern France start with 03, mobile phones start with 06 and numbers starting 08 indicate a variety of special rate numbers, varying from 0800 freephones to 0892 premium rates. Phone boxes generally require *télécartes* (telephone cards) which can be bought at post offices, tobacconists and some supermarkets. Directory enquiries are available from various providers, all starting with 118, including 118000, 118007, 118008 and 118218 or look at the website ⓦ www.pagesjaunes.fr

Post

There are several post offices around town including branches on place Drouet d'Erlon and rue Cérès. However, if you're just sending letters or postcards, it's usually quicker and simpler to buy stamps at a *tabac* (tobacconist). You can also use the automatic machines inside post offices. Letter boxes are bright yellow and are usually easy to spot.

ELECTRICITY
French electricity is 220 volts, 50 Hz AC. British visitors will need an adaptor (*adaptateur*); American visitors will need a transformer (*transformateur*).

TRAVELLERS WITH DISABILITIES
Newer hotels and restaurants generally have specially adapted rooms and toilets but disabled travellers may have trouble with older buildings; there are wheelchair accessible lifts at the Gare de Reims and Champagne-Ardenne train stations (see page 48).

TOURIST INFORMATION
Office de Tourisme de Reims Located next to the cathedral in the house of the medieval chapter treasurer, the tourist office can supply town maps and information on sights, accommodation and restaurants and organises guided visits; it also has an online accommodation booking service. ⓐ 2 rue Guillaume de Machault ⓣ 03 26 77 45 00 / 08 92 70 13 51 ⓦ www.reims-tourisme.com ⓛ 09.00–19.00 Mon–Sat, 09.00–18.00 Sun, summer; 09.00–18.00 Mon–Sat, 10.00–13.00 Sun, winter
Mairie de Reims (municipal website) ⓦ www.ville-reims.fr
Tourist information on the Marne region
ⓦ www.tourisme-en-champagne.com

Tourist information on the Champagne-Ardenne region
ⓦ www.tourisme-champagne-ardenne.com
Maison de la France (French national tourist board)
ⓦ www.franceguide.com

BACKGROUND READING

Rimbaud: The Double Life of a Rebel by Edmund White. Perceptive and intriguing study of the character who unwittingly – so it's just about possible to forgive him – inspired more than one rock star 'poet'.

The Second Battle of the Marne by Michael S Neilberg. This gripping account of the sole occasion on which British, American and French armies joined forces in World War I explains the pivotal battle of its final phase.

The Widow Clicquot: The Story of a Champagne Empire and the Woman Who Ruled It by Tilar J. Mazzeo. Who needs widow's weeds when you can draw up a business plan that will transform you into one of the founders of the modern Champagne industry?

Emergencies

The following are emergency free-call numbers:

Ambulance (*Samu*) ⓘ 15

Fire (*Sapeurs-Pompiers*) ⓘ 18

Police ⓘ 17

All emergency services from a mobile phone ⓘ 112

Note that the *sapeurs-pompiers* (fire brigade) also deals with medical emergencies

SOS Help (English-language helpline) ⓘ 01 46 21 46 46

🕐 15.00–23.00

MEDICAL SERVICES

CHU Reims (Centre Hospitalier Universitaire) ⓘ 03 26 78 78 78

Urgences (casualty) Hôpital Maison Blanche ⓐ 45 rue Cognacq Jay

ⓘ 03 26 78 76 02 🌐 www.chu-reims.fr ⓝ Bus: A, N

Urgences Enfants (children's casualty) American Memorial Hospital ⓐ 49 rue Cognacq Jay ⓘ 03 26 78 75 21 ⓝ Bus: A

Pharmacies de Garde (duty chemists) ⓘ 3237

SOS Médecins (medical advice by phone and house calls)

ⓘ 08 21 21 15 15

Centre Anti-Poisons (Lille) ⓘ 08 25 81 28 22

Centre Anti-Poisons (Nancy) ⓘ 03 83 32 36 36

POLICE

Crimes or theft should be reported to the police.

Hôtel de Police ⓐ 40 blvd Louis Roederer ⓘ 03 26 61 44 00

🕐 24 hrs

EMERGENCY PHRASES

Help!	**Fire!**	**Stop!**
Au secours!	Au feu!	Stop!
Ossercoor!	*Oh fur!*	*Stop!*

Call an ambulance/a doctor/the police/the fire service!
Appelez une ambulance/un médecin/la police/les pompiers!
*Ahperleh ewn ahngbewlahngss/ang medesang/
lah poleess/leh pompeeyeh!*

EMBASSIES & CONSULATES

If you lose your passport or have it stolen you should contact
your embassy's consular services in Paris.

American Consulate @ 2 rue St-Florentin, 75001 Paris
📞 01 43 12 22 22

Australian Embassy @ 4 rue Jean-Rey, 75015 Paris
📞 01 40 59 33 00

British Consulate @ 18 bis rue d'Anjou, 75008 Paris
📞 01 44 51 31 02

Canadian Embassy @ 35 av. Montaigne, 75008 Paris
📞 01 44 43 29 00

Irish Consulate @ 4 rue Rude, 75016 Paris 📞 01 44 17 67 00

New Zealand Embassy @ 7ter rue Léonard de Vinci, 75016 Paris
📞 01 45 01 43 43

South African Embassy @ 59 quai d'Orsay, 75007 Paris
📞 01 53 59 23 23

Send your thoughts to
books@thomascook.com

- Found a great bar, club, shop or must-see sight that we don't feature?
- Like to tip us off about any information that needs a little updating?
- Want to tell us what you love about this handy little guidebook and more importantly how we can make it even handier?

Then here's your chance to tell all! Send us ideas, discoveries and recommendations today and then look out for your valuable input in the next edition of this title.

Email the above address (stating the title) or write to:
CitySpots Series Editor, Thomas Cook Publishing, PO Box 227, Coningsby Road, Peterborough PE3 8SB, UK.

SPOTTED YOUR NEXT CITY BREAK?

...then these lightweight CitySpots pocket guides will have you in the know in no time, wherever you're heading.

Covering over 90 cities worldwide, they're packed with detail on the most important urban attractions from shopping and sights to non-stop nightlife; knocking spots off chunkier, clunkier versions.

Aarhus	Gdansk	Oslo
Amsterdam	Geneva	Palermo
Antwerp	Genoa	Palma
Athens	Glasgow	Paris
Bangkok	Gothenburg	Pisa
Barcelona	Granada	Prague
Belfast	Hamburg	Porto
Belgrade	Hanover	Reykjavik
Berlin	Helsinki	Riga
Biarritz	Hong Kong	Rome
Bilbao	Istanbul	Rotterdam
Bologna	Kiev	Salzburg
Bordeaux	Krakow	Sarajevo
Bratislava	Kuala Lumpur	Seville
Bruges	Leipzig	Singapore
Brussels	Lille	Sofia
Bucharest	Lisbon	Stockholm
Budapest	Liverpool	Strasbourg
Cairo	Ljubljana	St Petersburg
Cape Town	London	Tallinn
Cardiff	Los Angeles	Tirana
Cologne	Lyon	Tokyo
Copenhagen	Madrid	Toulouse
Cork	Marrakech	Turin
Dubai	Marseilles	Valencia
Dublin	Milan	Venice
Dubrovnik	Monte Carlo	Verona
Düsseldorf	Moscow	Vienna
Edinburgh	Munich	Vilnius
Fez	Naples	Warsaw
Florence	New York City	Zagreb
Frankfurt	Nice	Zurich

Editorial/project management: Lisa Plumridge
Copy editor: Paul Hines
Layout/DTP: Alison Rayner

The publishers would like to thank the following individuals and organisations for supplying their copyright photographs for this book: A L'Instant T/JTL, page 125; Christophe Alary, page 45; Gavin Anderson, page 117; Dennis Beentjes, pages 40–1; Daniel Cartwright, page 31; Natasha Edwards, pages 43, 47, 59, 65, 87, 89, 92, 99, 101, 119 & 122; Everjean, page 15; Fotolia.com (Jerome Delahaye, pages 7 & 57; ploum1, page 27); Groupe Bombaron, pages 35 & 38; Yagil Henkin, page 1; Late Night Venture, page 32; Jean Lemoine, page 81; David Máška, page 23; Maza, page 129; Mind On Fire, page 11; James Mitchell, page 9; mpd01605, pages 73 & 127; mx.style, page 49; Zoe Rimmer, page 21; Jean-Pierre Riocreux, page 19; Colin Rose, pages 66, 76 & 95; Pascal Ruyskart, page 105; Soundsnaps/Dreamstime.com, page 107; Bram Van Damme, page 110.